My Dear Holmes

My Dear Holmes

A STUDY IN SHERLOCK

GAVIN BREND

OTTO
PENZLER
BOOKS

NEW YORK

This edition is reprinted by arrangement with HarperCollins Publishers.

Otto Penzler Books, 129 West 56th Street,
New York, NY 10019 (Editorial Offices only)

Macmillan Publishing Company, 866 Third Avenue,
New York, NY 10022

Maxwell Macmillan Canada, Inc., 1200 Eglinton Avenue East,
Suite 200, Don Mills, Ontario M3C 3N1

Macmillan Publishing Company is part of the Maxwell
Communication Group of Companies.

Library of Congress Cataloging-in-Publication Data
Brend, Gavin.
  My dear Holmes: a study in Sherlock / by Gavin Brend.
    p.   cm.
  Originally published: London: Allen & Unwin, 1951.
  Includes bibliographical references (p.   ).
  ISBN 1-883402-69-7
  1. Doyle, Arthur Conan, Sir, 1859–1930—Characters—Sherlock
Holmes. 2. Detective and mystery stories, English—History and
criticism. Holmes, Sherlock (Fictitious character). 4. Private
investigators in literature. I. Title.
PR4624.B74   1994   93-42878   CIP
823'.8—dc20

10 9 8 7 6 5 4 3 2 1

Printed in the United States of America

The Second Stain

The Solitary Cyclist

The Dancing Men

The Speckled Band

The Reigate Squire

The Boscombe Valley Mystery

The Red-Headed League

The Norwood Builder

The Abbey Grange

The Final Problem

A reverie

Preface

❦

MR. HESKETH PEARSON in his biography of Sir Arthur
Conan Doyle has pointed out that there are only four
characters in English literature who have achieved
universal fame. Others may be known to the literate
and the semi-literate but only these four can be certain
of recognition by millions who have never read a line
of the works in which they appear. The four are Romeo,
Shylock, Robinson Crusoe and Sherlock Holmes.

One feels that even if one of the first three had had
the good fortune to have lived in St. Marylebone, it is
highly doubtful whether that borough's enterprising
Council would have been deluged by a flood of correspondence demanding that a special exhibition should
be held in his honour as part of the 1951 Festival of
Britain. Nor do I imagine that Juliet or Antonio or Man
Friday would write a letter to *The Times* about it. It is
only with Sherlock Holmes that these things could
happen.

But in spite of his world-wide fame there are many
aspects of Holmes's life on which Watson leaves us in
complete ignorance, and he is even more reticent about
some of his own affairs. When was Holmes born?
Which university did he go to and how long was he
there? Whereabouts in Baker Street did he reside? Did
he ever go to Tibet? What exactly was the Sherlock
Holmes Agency? How many times was Watson married
and in what years? Why was he absent from Baker
Street in 1896? Who was the mysterious lady who
married him in 1902 and about whom we know so
little? Why is he blessed with a superfluity of Chris-

tian names whilst in the Moriarty family there is a shortage?

These are the sort of problems which confront us when we read Watson's narratives for the second time. On the first occasion we are too interested in the problems which Holmes actually solves to worry about these others. Reading them again, however, we approach the matter from a different angle.

For me (and I think for many others) the trouble started with Watson's first marriage. Some of his cases purport to have taken place in particular years, others are merely dated by reference to this marriage. It seemed, therefore, desirable to ascertain the date of the marriage. But this was not so easy as it sounds. The pieces in this elaborate jig-saw puzzle refused to fit. Dates had to be altered. Reasons had to be found for altering the dates. New mysteries came to light demanding a solution. Before long I came to the conclusion that the only way to unravel the tangle was to write Holmes's life. Hence this book.

Faced with this conflict of dates I recall that Mr. Vincent Starrett has described the Baker Street of Sherlock Holmes as a fascinating country of the mind, which never existed in reality, where time has no meaning and it is always 1895. No doubt this is sheer escapism, but I must confess that for me a world in which it is always 1895 is not without its attractions. I would therefore like to put forward two completely contradictory excuses for this book; first that it is an endeavour to sort out the conflicting tangle of dates and secondly that I cannot resist writing about events which are 'always 1895.'

In conclusion I would like to acknowledge my indebtedness to my many predecessors. Biographies of

Holmes have been written by Mr. H. H. Bell and Mr. T. S. Blakeney, and of Watson by Mr. S. C. Roberts. Others who have written about them include Monsignor Ronald Knox, Miss Dorothy Sayers, Mr. A. G. Macdonell, Sir Desmond MacCarthy, Mr. Vernon Rendall, Mr. Vincent Starrett and Mr. Christopher Morley. The research which they have carried out has made my task easier and even where I am at complete variance with their conclusions my indebtedness to them is not in any way diminished.

I should also like to express my gratitude to Mr. E. L. Hawke of the Royal Meteorological Society for supplying me with information as to February snowfalls in the eighties for the purpose of establishing the date of *The Beryl Coronet*.

CONTENTS

ILLUSTRATIONS

CHAPTER ONE

Master Sherlock

HISTORY has little to tell us of the early years in the life of Sherlock Holmes. Watson, unfortunately, was too absorbed in the long pageant of sensational cases which succeeded each other with kaleidoscopic rapidity to have any time left to investigate his subject's early days.

Thus neither the date nor the place of his birth have been recorded. So far as the latter is concerned we can only guess. Could it perhaps have been somewhere on the South Downs where he retired to keep bees in his old age? We shall never know.

But if nothing can be said about the place, quite a lot can be said about the date. In fact, unless we are to eschew dates entirely, any biography of Holmes becomes a succession of elaborate conjuring tricks with the years. The date of his birth is but the first of these. We start at a late stage in his career and work backwards until we reach his birth.

The starting point is the case of *The Creeping Man*, the date of which is September 1903. Watson says that this was 'one of the very last cases handled by Holmes.' It can be assumed therefore that he retired at the end of 1903.

Next we come to *The Veiled Lodger* in which we are told that 'Mr. Sherlock Holmes was in active practice for twenty-three years.' This period of twenty-three years was not, however, continuous. Owing to the activities of the Moriarty organization there was a break which started at the end of April, 1891[1] and continued for a period of slightly less than three years.[2] During these three years Holmes was certainly not inactive,[3] but as he was away from Baker Street for the whole three years he can scarcely be said to have been 'in active practice.' Accordingly his career would appear to comprise the thirteen years 1878-1890, both years inclusive, and the ten years 1894-1903, both inclusive.

The earliest case in this period of '*active* practice' is *The Musgrave Ritual*. Prior to that only two clients had come his way, but thereafter things improved, so that by the time he met Watson in 1881 he had 'established a considerable, though not a very lucrative connection.' *The Musgrave Ritual* can therefore be dated 1878.

Musgrave who introduced the case was a college acquaintance, and we are told by Holmes that 'for four years I had seen nothing of him.' Holmes was therefore at college in the year 1874. In fact it was his third year there, but as the evidence required to establish this statement is somewhat lengthy, it will be convenient to defer the explanation until a later stage.[4] Here we will merely state that he started his college career in 1871.

Since most undergraduates start at the age of eighteen it would seem that the most likely year for his birth would be 1853.

One further item of evidence is available. In *His Last Bow*, Altamont, alias Holmes, was on August 2, 1914, described as 'a tall, gaunt man of sixty.' Presumably 'sixty' is no more than an approximate

---

[1] *The Final Problem.*   [2] *The Empty House.*
[3] See Chapter XI.   [4] See Chapter III.

estimate at a round figure, and if so this would seem to agree fairly closely with the above statement.

Of his family little is known. He once informed Watson[1] that his ancestors were for the most part country squires of no particular distinction. But his grandmother was a Vernet, a sister of one of the well-known French painters of that family. It is probable that her brother was Horace Vernet (1789–1863) and her father Carle Vernet (1758–1835), though it would be possible for her to be the sister of Carle and the daughter of Claude Joseph Vernet (1714–1789).

It seems that one branch of the Vernet family settled in England and, as Mr. Roberts has pointed out, the name subsequently became anglicized to Verner. It was a doctor of that name who purchased Watson's practice in Kensington in 1894, thus enabling him to rejoin Holmes in Baker Street after the Moriarty episode. The purchase price was surprisingly high, and it was not until some time later that Watson discovered that Verner was in fact a distant relation of Holmes and that it was Holmes who had actually financed him.[2]

Apart from Dr. Verner the only other relation of Holmes known to us is his brother Mycroft who was born seven years before Sherlock.

It is a great pity that we have no record of young Sherlock's schooldays. Was he an infant prodigy, or did his remarkable powers develop later in his life? Alas, there was no Watson present to tell us. We cannot help wondering whether his schoolmasters occupied a somewhat similar role to that of the unfortunate Scotland Yard team in his later life. In any event one feels that he cannot have been a very easy pupil.

[1] *The Greek Interpreter.*   [2] *The Norwood Builder.*

CHAPTER TWO

Oxford or Cambridge

PROBABLY he was not sorry when the time came for him to go to the University. At all events we are not sorry, for this immediately raises a highly controversial problem. Which university? The minor ones can be ruled out at once. Brief as it is, the reference in *The 'Gloria Scott'*[1] clearly points to either Oxford or Cambridge. Nor does the languid aristocratic Musgrave, associated with 'grey archways and mullioned windows and all the venerable wreckage of a feudal keep' sound the sort of undergraduate whom one would expect to find at one of the lesser universities in the seventies.

Oxford or Cambridge it must be then. But which? Monsignor Ronald Knox says Christ Church, Oxford.[2] Miss Sayers says Sidney Sussex, Cambridge.[3] Mr. Blakeney also says Cambridge, but does not nominate any particular college.[4]

So far as the college is concerned there seems to be no real evidence available. We rather think that he was at St. Luke's, the scene of *The Three Students*, but this does not help, for we are specifically told that no details are given which might enable us to identify the college.

[1] See pages 26–27.
[2] 'Studies in the Literature of Sherlock Holmes' in *Essays in Satire*.
[3] 'Holmes's College Career,' in *Baker Street Studies*.
[4] *Sherlock Holmes: Fact or Fiction?*

In attempting to solve the Oxford *v.* Cambridge problem it is necessary to consider five separate cases which in some form or other refer to University affairs. On examination these five fall into three distinct categories as follows:

Group 1: *The 'Gloria Scott'* and *The Musgrave Ritual.*

Group 2: *The Missing Three-Quarter.*

Group 3: *The Three Students* and *The Creeping Man.*

In the first group we know that we are at Holmes's university though we do not know whether it be Oxford or Cambridge, in the second group we know that we are at Cambridge, but are ignorant as to whether or not it is Holmes's university, whilst in the third group we have no information on either point.

All previous research seems to have concentrated almost exclusively on Group 1. It is perhaps not surprising that Group 3 has been overlooked, but there is surely a profitable field to cultivate in Group 2. In other words since we know that in *The Missing Three-Quarter* we are at Cambridge, what is the evidence that Holmes had ever been there before? Let us start our investigation at this point.

In the first place he does not know that there is a late train from London to Cambridge. When Godfrey Staunton, the Rugby international, who must not of course be confused with either Arthur H. Staunton, 'the rising young forger' or Henry Staunton 'whom I helped to hang,' disappears from the hotel in London in which the Cambridge team are staying on the eve of the Oxford match, Cyril Overton, the captain of the team comes to consult Holmes and is asked by him whether Staunton could have got back to Cambridge. The reply is that he could, as there is a late train at quarter past eleven.

Now Holmes in his own college days was residing in London.[1] One would have thought, therefore, that if his University was Cambridge he would know approximately the time of the last train. It may be, however, in this particular case, that the difficulty can be removed by assuming that this late train was not in existence in Holmes's time but was first put on at some later date.

After some enquiries in London, Holmes and Watson travel up to Cambridge and though they are clearly in a train which is much earlier than the aforesaid 11.15 p.m., it is nevertheless dark by the time they get there. On arrival they immediately interview Dr. Leslie Armstrong who is suspected of being involved in Staunton's disappearance. The next problem is to find rooms for the night and in this connection Holmes says :

'And now, my poor Watson, here we are, stranded and friendless, in this inhospitable town, which we cannot leave without abandoning our case.'

Why 'this inhospitable town'? Is not this a remark which is far more applicable to the town of the rival University than to one's own? Does not this read like disparagement of Cambridge by an Oxonian? It may be objected that Holmes was not a typical representative of Cambridge, that he was an aloof reserved sort of fellow who went his own way and that such a one might well take a somewhat jaundiced view of the town. But surely if that were the case he would make some further reference to his own period of residence there. He would say 'this inhospitable town which even in my own day I always disliked intensely' or some such phrase. But 'this inhospitable town' with no

[1] *The 'Gloria Scott.'*

further addition reads like the remark of a man who is visiting the town for the first time.

Fortunately there is a small inn situated conveniently opposite to Armstrong's house and before long the doctor's carriage is seen emerging and Holmes is off in pursuit on a bicycle leaving Watson behind at the inn. But the pursuit is abortive. Holmes is detected by the doctor who stops and calls his bluff. On his return Watson suggests that the shadowing should be continued next day but is met with the retort:

'It is not so easy as you seem to think. You are not familiar with Cambridgeshire scenery, are you? It does not lend itself to concealment. All this country that I passed over to-night is as flat and clean as the palm of your hand.'

But in that case why did Holmes ever undertake a pursuit which was foredoomed to failure? The answer would appear to be that having never been in Cambridge before he was in the same state of lamentable ignorance as to the distinctive peculiarities of Cambridgeshire scenery. We now see the significance of Watson's remark that it was after dark when they first arrived in Cambridge. Had they arrived in daylight, Holmes would have seen the difficulties from the window of his train, but as it was, they only became apparent after he had actually started out. Armstrong may well have been aided by a moon which had not risen or was obscured by cloud when they first entered Cambridge.

Realizing that shadowing Armstrong is not a practical proposition, Holmes devotes the next day to an enquiry in the pubs to the north of Cambridge, visiting without success 'Chesterton, Histon, Waterbeach and Oakington.'

Note the order, for it is a rather peculiar one. Presumably he visited them in the order in which he names them, particularly in view of the certainty that in any circumstances Chesterton would obviously come first. But consider the position of the other three. From Cambridge or from Chesterton, Histon lies to the north-west, Oakington is still further north-west, but Waterbeach is to the north-east. So that if he went to Waterbeach after Histon he would probably come back again through Histon in order to get to Oakington. The obvious route which anyone familiar with the neighbourhood would take would be Chesterton, Waterbeach, Histon, Oakington, and the route actually taken reveals the Oxonian in a hurry who has not yet had time to procure a map.

By the next day however it seems that this error has been remedied for he has heard of Trumpington. But what are his actual words as the draghound leads him to the village in which Godfrey Staunton is finally run to earth?

'This *should be* the village of Trumpington to the right of us.'

He could hardly have been at Cambridge without visiting a place so near. The Cantab would certainly say 'This *is* Trumpington.' The 'should be' is the mark of the Oxonian. So too we suggest is the expression 'the village of Trumpington' as opposed to mere 'Trumpington.' The former suggests the stranger, the latter the neighbour.

It seems to us therefore that *The Missing Three-Quarter* points unmistakably to Oxford. We must next consider how far the two cases in Group 3 support this view.

In dealing with *The Three Students* the first thing is to

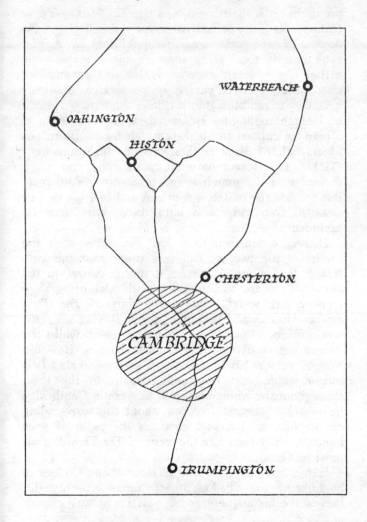

prove that it is slightly earlier than *The Missing Three-Quarter*. *The Three Students* we know is dated 1895. *The Missing Three-Quarter* was first published in August 1904 and it took place some seven or eight years earlier. At a later stage[1] we give our reasons for selecting 1897 as the year in question. Here it is only necessary to establish that it is later than 1895. It must be later than 1893 for Holmes speaks of Armstrong as a man 'calculated to fill the gap left by the illustrious Moriarty.' It took place therefore after his return from 'Tibet.' This leaves only the years 1894 and 1895. Oxford won the match owing to Staunton's absence. But in 1894 the match was drawn and in 1895 victory went to Cambridge. So both these years must be excluded.

Having established that *The Three Students* is the earlier of the two we can now prove that this case relates to Oxford. We refer to the sentence quoted above 'You are not familiar with Cambridgeshire scenery, are you?' Now at the start of *The Three Students* Holmes and Watson had been staying 'for some weeks in one of our great University towns' whilst the former was studying Early English charters. How did Watson occupy his time during these few weeks? It is inconceivable that he would remain in the town throughout the whole period. If he were in Cambridge he would be bound to know about the surrounding countryside 'as flat and clean as the palm of your hand.' Clearly therefore the scene of *The Three Students* must be Oxford.

Hilton Soames, tutor and lecturer at the College of St. Luke's, is described as 'an acquaintance.' Where did they make his acquaintance? Was he by any chance

[1] See pages 153–154.

a survivor from Holmes's own undergraduate days whom Holmes had taken the opportunity to contact on his return to Oxford? At all events Soames knows that he is in Oxford and when it is discovered that the Fortescue Scholarship examination paper has been read by an unauthorized person, Soames knows what to do about it.

'You are aware, Mr. Holmes, that our college doors are double—a green baize one within and a heavy oak one without.'

Why should Holmes be aware of this? Is the answer that he himself was a St. Luke's man?

By the time Holmes has finished his enquiries it is evening and darkness had fallen, but he knows that there are only four stationers of any consequence in Oxford, and he also knows where each one is located and has time to visit all four before they close for the night.

An even more remarkable demonstration of local knowledge follows. Holmes and Watson are together until bedtime that day and Watson is up at eight o'clock next morning. But Holmes has forestalled him by two hours during which he has been out to the athletic grounds to collect some black clay and sawdust from the jumping-pit.

How did he know his way there? Watson is a witness to the fact that he could not have got this information on the previous day and at six in the morning hardly anybody would be astir. Yet he *does* know where to go. It may be objected that on his own showing, he was not interested in athletics during his University career and that his sports were boxing and fencing. Nevertheless, we think that he knew far more about what was going on around him than he pretended, and that the attitude of aloofness was to some extent a pose. We frequently find that he, in fact, knows more than he admits, and if he were to state that he did not know where the athletic grounds were we should treat this with the same reserve as his famous statement that he did not know or care whether the sun went round the earth or vice versa.

We now come to the case of *The Creeping Man* which adds very little to our information. As Holmes proposes to 'enjoy the amenities of this charming town' it is evidently not 'the inhospitable town' of *The Missing Three-Quarter*. There is also a reference to driving past a row of ancient colleges, and whilst at a pinch this might be King's Parade of Trinity Street in Cambridge, colleges in rows, on the whole, suggest Oxford.

So far wherever a university has been specifically mentioned it is Cambridge, wherever it has been left anonymous, on investigation it turns out to be Oxford. As Holmes's own university comes in this latter category one would anticipate that it too would prove to be Oxford.

There now only remain to be considered the two cases in Group 1 which refer to Holmes's own college days, namely *The 'Gloria Scott'* and *The Musgrave Ritual*.

Mr. Blakeney suggests that Trevor of *The 'Gloria Scott,'* being a Norfolk man, would find it more convenient to send his son to Cambridge than to Oxford. Against this may be set Monsignor Knox's firm belief that the exclusive aristocracy of Musgrave and the doggy tendencies of Trevor indicate that all three were at Christ Church. These two arguments may be left to cancel each other out.

We now come to the incident of Miss Dorothy Sayers's bull-terrier, or to be more accurate Victor

Trevor's bull-terrier. The relevant passage from *The 'Gloria Scott'* is as follows:

'He (Victor Trevor) was the only friend I made during the two years that I was at college. I was never a very sociable fellow, Watson, always rather fond of moping in my rooms and working out my own little methods of thought, so that I never mixed much with the men of my year. Bar fencing and boxing I had few athletic tastes, and then my line of study was quite distinct from that of the other fellows, so that we had no points of contact at all. Trevor was the only man I knew, and that only through the accident of his bull-terrier freezing on to my ankle one morning as I went down to chapel.'

It is open to argument whether or not Holmes's college career was limited to two years. This will be discussed at a later stage. What however is clear is that this incident of the dog must have occurred within two years of his arrival. On the strength of this Miss Sayers produces an ingenious theory in support of Cambridge. Dogs are not allowed inside the college gates at either university, therefore the incident must have happened out in the street. At Cambridge undergraduates usually spend their first two years in rooms, moving into college thereafter. At Oxford the reverse is the case. This incident happened in the first two years, therefore it must have happened at Cambridge.

But this assumes that the rules are always obeyed. Is this quite the picture that one has of either Oxford or Cambridge? Could not the dog have been smuggled into the college for the purpose of some practical joke? Alternatively, from the standpoint of the dog, could not the event happen both outside and inside the college? Why should it not have been frightened or hurt out in the street with the result that before it could be stopped it ran through the gate and fastened on to the unfortunate Holmes? What could be simpler?

Finally there remains an argument which has been put forward on behalf of Cambridge which is of a general character and is not dependent on any one case. It is said that with his bent for science, Cambridge would be the obvious choice.

There might be some force in this argument if his interests were confined to science. But in point of fact he happens to have had an extensive knowledge of literature, history, philosophy, art and music, spoke at least three foreign languages and was in fact a complete walking encyclopaedia. Moreover it seems probable that his scientific knowledge was not acquired at his university since we find him at a later stage studying at Barts.

To sum up therefore we think that whilst the bull-terrier makes a valiant effort on behalf of Cambridge, the verdict must be given to Oxford.

CHAPTER THREE

Before Baker Street

THE bull-terrier, though he did not know it, was making history. His interest in Holmes's ankle, unfortunate on a short term view, ultimately had entirely beneficial results, as it started the chain of events that led up to his choice of a career. He was laid up for ten days during which a contrite Trevor came to visit him. Soon they had become close friends and Trevor invited him to his home at Donnithorpe in Norfolk early in the long vacation.

It was there that the case of *The 'Gloria Scott'* occurred which years later Holmes was to narrate to Watson round the fire on a winter's night in Baker Street. The young undergraduate succeeded in decoding the mysterious message relating to fly-papers and hen pheasants and it was this success which first suggested to him that he might devote his life to the detection and prevention of crime; to act as a final court of appeal when all the resources of Scotland Yard had failed.

To ascertain the year of *The 'Gloria Scott'* case we must look forward. For the moment all that we need bear in mind is that it took place in the middle seventies since we have already shown[1] that Holmes's period of active practice began in 1878. If instead of looking forward we look backward we encounter that grizzly

[1] See page 2.

nightmare, the original voyage of the *Gloria Scott*. Of all the many mysteries with which we are confronted, this is beyond all doubt the most insoluble. From the standpoint of fixing a date it is really a waste of time to embark once more on this voyage with the elder Trevor. But let us nevertheless do so.

He tells us that the voyage took place thirty years earlier in 1855 when the Crimean War was at its height and the Government had been compelled to use their larger convict ships to transport troops to the Black Sea, thus being left with only the smaller and less suitable ships such as the *Gloria Scott* for the convicts. If this were correct the date of *The 'Gloria Scott'* would be 1885. This however is manifestly impossible in any circumstances whatsoever.

The obvious solution at first sight appears to be the substitution of twenty years for thirty. This however merely lands us in new difficulties, for the exasperating Trevor senior, not content with saying that the voyage took place thirty years ago must needs also tell us that he returned to England as a rich colonial more than twenty years ago. The wretch therefore forces us to make a corresponding reduction of ten years in this twenty year period.

A further difficulty is his age. As if he had not done enough harm already, he tells us that he was twenty-three years of age at the time of the voyage. Yet Holmes refers to him on more than one occasion as an old man. It is bad enough if this description is applied to a man aged fifty-three, but it is the last straw when it is applied to one of forty-three.

And Trevor junior's age? If he were old enough to be at Oxford, his father must have married before the ill-fated voyage. Perhaps he did. Research into his family history discloses only that at the end of his life he was a widower, and the tragic but completely irrelevant fact that there had been a daughter who died of diphtheria while on a visit to Birmingham.

As this line of approach seems fairly hopeless another possibility is to assume that 1855 is an error for 1845. This certainly gives us a relatively coherent story so far as Trevor is concerned. But what then becomes of the Crimea and of the troopships? Nor are our difficulties made any easier by Holmes's insistence that the document which he read to Watson was no copy but the actual original which he received from Victor Trevor.

Mr. Bell suggests[1] that the whole story is a tissue of lies invented by Trevor to forestall Hudson and to whitewash himself in his son's eyes. He was probably a murderer and a pirate who was being blackmailed by his confederate Hudson.

But whilst we can well believe that he would be capable of any infamy, we do not see how this explains the chaotic muddle of dates. There seems to be no alternative therefore but to write off the whole incident and to endeavour to date the case of *The 'Gloria Scott'* as distinct from the voyage by some other means.

It seems clear that Holmes was destined to return to Oxford after his visit to Donnithorpe, for at that time he was still talking about the long vacation. Moreover, the Holmes of *The 'Gloria Scott'* was 'fond of moping in my rooms and working out my own little methods of thought, so that I never mixed much with the men of my year.' But the Holmes of *The Musgrave Ritual* was a different sort of person, for 'during my last years at the university there was a good deal of talk there about myself and my methods,' and Musgrave asks him if he

[1] *Sherlock Holmes and Doctor Watson.*

is 'turning to practical ends the powers with which you used to amaze us.'

Clearly then his experiences at Donnithorpe had made all the difference. He had acquired new confidence in his methods. Hitherto his audience had consisted solely of his one intimate friend, Victor Trevor. Now there burst forth on an astonished Oxford those experiments in observation and deduction which in later years were to astonish Watson, Scotland Yard and his clients.

Further it is evident that he had still at least two years to do, as these experiments took place 'during my last years.' Now this at first seems to conflict with the passage previously quoted from *The 'Gloria Scott'* that Trevor 'was the only friend I had made during the two years I was at college' which of course implies a total college career of two years. The explanation must be that Holmes actually said 'up to the time of the case of which I am now about to tell you he was the only friend I had made during my two years at college,' and that Watson made an inadequate note of this conversation which resulted in the omission of the first part of the sentence when he ultimately wrote his account of the case.

The requirement therefore is a four-year period of which the first two are before and the last two after the vacation at Donnithorpe. To obtain these years we must consider the college career of Richard Musgrave of 'the thin high nose, the large eyes and the languid yet courtly manners.'

As we have already shown, Holmes started his active professional career in 1878, this being the year of *The Musgrave Ritual* in which he tells us that four years had passed since he last saw Musgrave. This means that

Musgrave could not have left Oxford before 1874. He could have left after that year on the assumption that Holmes left in 1874 but this is unlikely as apparently he had become M.P. for his district some time before 1878. Progress in a political career at this speed is very exceptional and we are therefore entitled to assume that he left at the earliest possible date, i.e. 1874.

As Miss Sayers shrewdly observes, we can conclude that Holmes and Musgrave were in the same year, for if the latter were the senior, his reserved and somewhat exclusive manner which was in fact due to diffidence, would have precluded him from associating with a mere freshman. We know too that he was at Oxford after the Donnithorpe vacation as he refers to the experiments 'with which you used to amaze us.' But whereas Holmes was up for two years after Donnithorpe, Musgrave may have been up for only one. In other words if Musgrave went down, as he did in 1874, Holmes may have gone down in either 1874 or 1875.

In deciding between these two years we have to consider Holmes's temperament and the events (or rather lack of events) of the next years. We know that *The Musgrave Ritual* was his third case. Before that came a long weary period in which there were only two cases when 'I waited, filling in my too abundant leisure time by studying all those branches of science which might make me more efficient.' This period must in any case have been about two-and-a-half years, and if he started in 1874 an extra year must be added. It is unlikely that a man of Holmes's energy could have endured three-and-a-half years of idleness. He would have concluded that he had made a mistake, and would have abandoned his original choice for a more lucrative profession. We suggest that two-and-a-half years might be taken as the extreme limit of his patience and that the other year must in fact have been passed at college, in other words, that his fourth and last year at college was 1875.

It would seem therefore that the relevant dates are as follows:—

1871 Holmes goes to Oxford.

1873 Vacation at Donnithorpe. The case of *The 'Gloria Scott.'*

1874 Musgrave leaves Oxford.

1875 Holmes leaves Oxford.

There was now no doubt as to his future career. He took rooms in Montague Street 'just round the corner from the British Museum' and was presumably still there at the time when he first met Watson. Of the only two cases that came his way between 1875 and 1878 we know nothing, except that they were both introduced by old fellow-students who had been impressed by his demonstrations at Oxford. But certain inferences of a negative character can be made about these cases. We can be reasonably certain that they were not of a very sensational or dramatic nature, and that they did not supply Holmes with the raw material that he needed to exhibit those powers of deduction which figured in so many of his later cases. It is possible, though less certain, that they did not involve intervention by the police. (Of the sixty cases reported by Watson about one-fifth appear to have been solved by Holmes without the police becoming aware of their existence.)

Early in the year 1878 there came at last the case for which Holmes had waited so long. *The Musgrave Ritual* supplied all the elements which the previous cases had lacked. It is true that the murderer of butler Brunton was never brought to book. But Holmes did at least succeed in unearthing the body from its strange hiding place, thus establishing that a murder had been committed, and at the same time he decoded the famous Ritual message, a message which at first seemed even more inexplicable than the hen pheasants of *The 'Gloria Scott.'*

From that time onwards neither Scotland Yard nor the world at large could afford to ignore him. Clients began to arrive though they were not always as plentiful nor as lucrative as they might have been.

The distinction of being the first client other than a former member of Oxford University to consult Sherlock Holmes is, we believe, held by a certain Mrs. Farintosh. What this good lady's trouble was we shall never know. All that we know is that it was 'the hour of her sore need' and that 'it was concerned with an opal tiara.' Holmes himself had to refer to a small case-book before he could remember it.[1]

To this period too belonged the Tarleton murders, the case of Vamberry, the wine merchant, the adventure of the old Russian woman, the singular affair of the aluminium crutch and the case of Ricoletti of the club-foot and his abominable wife.[2] They were not all successes.

What was needed now was someone to keep a record of the cases for the benefit of posterity. As Holmes himself was to say on a later occasion 'I am lost without my Boswell.'[3] But this defect was soon to be remedied. Boswell was already knocking at the door.

[1] *The Speckled Band.*
[2] *The Musgrave Ritual.*
[3] *A Scandal in Bohemia.*

My Dear Watson

❧

To those who believe that the age of miracles is past, our usual reply is to produce a map of London on which we have marked (1) Barts, (2) The Criterion, and (3) all the places lying between Barts and the Criterion at which one can get a drink.

On a winter's morning in 1881 we have X working in the chemical laboratory at Barts and wondering where he can find someone to share some rooms which he has found in Baker Street; we have Y standing in the Criterion Bar and wondering where he can find some rooms which are less expensive than his present quarters and we have Z, also in Barts, who is not interested in the question of rooms at all, but is merely wondering where he will go for a drink before lunch. Z knows about X and his requirements. He knows Y too but has not seen him for some time. What are the odds against Z steering a straight and undeviating line from Barts to the Criterion Bar, avoiding all the pitfalls, false turnings and Vanity Fairs that lie strewn across his path and bringing Y back in triumph to Barts?

We should think it would be somewhat improbable to say the least of it, unless of course we have an equation in which X = Holmes, Y = Watson and Z = young Stamford, one of the great contact men of history.

At all events young Stamford did decide to go to the Criterion Bar for his aperitif and he encountered an old acquaintance for whom he had previously officiated as a dresser at Barts, one John H. Watson, whose military career had recently come to a close as a result of a Jezail bullet wound in the shoulder,[1] or the leg,[2] or both, followed by an attack of enteric fever at the base hospital at Peshawar. In the circumstances he can hardly be accused of exaggeration when he says that his wound occurred at 'the fatal battle of Maiwand.'

Watson took Stamford off to lunch at the Holborn and asked him during the meal whether he knew of any lodgings suitable for one whose purse was not his strongest point. Stamford at once proposed an adjournment to Barts. The great moment had at last arrived:

'Dr. Watson, Mr. Sherlock Holmes.'

What did they think of each other at first sight? Watson very soon after the meeting at Barts recorded his impressions of Holmes. Holmes about the same time gave a short description of Watson in order to explain how he knew that he had recently returned from Afghanistan. The two pen pictures make an interesting contrast. Here is Holmes as seen by Watson.

'In height he was rather over six feet, and so excessively lean that he seemed to be considerably taller. His eyes were sharp and piercing, save during the intervals of torpor to which I have alluded; and his thin hawk-like nose gave his whole expression an air of alertness and decision. His chin, too, had the prominence and squareness which mark the man of determination. His hands were invariably blotted with ink and stained with chemicals, yet he was possessed of extraordinary delicacy of touch . . .'

[1] *A Study in Scarlet.*   [2] *The Sign of Four.*

And here we have Watson as seen by Holmes.

'Here is a gentleman of a medical type, but with the air of a military man. Clearly an army doctor, then. He has just come from the tropics, for his face is dark, and that is not the natural tint of his skin, for his wrists are fair. He has undergone hardship and sickness, as his haggard face says clearly. His left arm has been injured. He holds it in a stiff and unnatural manner. Where in the tropics could an English army doctor have seen much hardship and got his arm wounded? Clearly in Afghanistan.'

So this strangely assorted pair set up house together in 221B Baker Street. As for Stamford, his mission in life accomplished, he fades for ever from our view. So far as our records are concerned neither Holmes nor Watson ever referred to him again. It was he who made Baker Street. Yet Baker Street knew him not. His last remark to Watson was prophetic. 'I'll wager he learns more about you than you do about him.'

It did indeed take Watson some considerable time to get to know Holmes. Whilst in some subjects such as chemistry Holmes was obviously brilliant, he appeared to be at first sight abysmally ignorant in others. Watson was so intrigued with these variations that he made an analysis of Holmes's knowledge, or lack of knowledge. The first two items, literature and philosophy, were both assessed as 'Nil.'

But in *The Sign of Four* alone we find Holmes either quoting or referring to Carlyle, Goethe, Jean Paul and Winwood Reade. He concludes *A Case of Identity* with the remark that there is as much sense in Hafiz as in Horace. In *The Boscombe Valley · Mystery* he reads Petrarch on a train journey and insists on talking about George Meredith when Watson wants to discuss the

case. He quotes Shakespeare in *The Red Circle* and elsewhere, Flaubert in *The Red-Headed League* and Thoreau
in *The Noble Bachelor*, and Mr. Vernon Rendall[1] has
unearthed three further quotations, all unacknow-
ledged, from Tacitus in *The Red-Headed League*, Boileau
in *A Study in Scarlet* and La Rochfoucauld in *The Sign
of Four*.

The reason for this very low literary assessment by
Watson seems to have been that Holmes had told him
in their very early days together that he had never
heard of Carlyle. We do not know the circumstances in
which this remark was made, but probably it was at a
time when Holmes wanted to give his whole attention
to a case, as yet unsolved, and simply could not be
bothered to be drawn into a discussion about Carlyle
or anything else. He had a time for everything and this
was *not* a time for a discussion on Carlyle.

He cannot have been an easy living companion.
Watson records in despair that he kept his cigars in the
coal-scuttle, his tobacco in a Persian slipper and his
unanswered correspondence transfixed by a jack-knife
to the centre of the mantelpiece.[2] The cigars and
tobacco might have escaped notice, but this cannot be
said of the jack-knife and as no visitor to Baker Street
ever appears to have made any comments it would
seem that this particular idiosyncrasy must have been
of short duration. Nor apparently was any visitor sufficiently indiscreet to comment on the V.R. pattern of
bullet marks on the wall. It would seem then that he
chose the sitting-room and not his own bedroom for
his exhibition of patriotic markmanship, for Watson,
not without justification, felt that neither the atmos-

[1] *The Limitations of Sherlock Holmes: Baker Street Studies.*
[2] *The Musgrave Ritual.*

phere nor the appearance of 'our room' were improved by it.

Then again there was his unfortunate addiction to cocaine. He was partaking of this as early as 1882[1] and by the beginning of 1887 his consumption had increased to three doses per day.[2] Watson then seems to have made a belated effort to effect a cure and Holmes was gradually weaned from the drug mania.[3] But in March 1897 he was ordered to take a rest as his health showed signs of breaking down, 'in the face of constant hard work of a most exacting kind, aggravated perhaps by occasional indiscretions of his own,'[4] and as late as December 1897 Watson had some anxiety lest the fiend was not dead but sleeping.[3] After that date there is no further reference to drugs. We can only conclude that the doses must have been much more dilute than Watson imagined they were, as they seem to have had little permanent ill effect upon his health at any time. Even the short enforced retirement in 1897 seems to have been due in the main to overwork rather than to drugs.

It is curious that in the first five years Watson should have made no attempt to effect a cure. He tells us[2] that although he often felt that he must protest, he lacked the courage to do so in the face of Holmes's cool, nonchalant manner, and so month after month passed by and he took no action. This inertia, which would be surprising in a layman, seems even more remarkable in a doctor. But then Watson was a very remarkable doctor.

In spite of certain indications to the contrary we believe that his heart was never at any time before

[1] *The Yellow Face.*   [2] *The Sign of Four.*
[3] *The Missing Three-Quarter.*   [4] *The Devil's Foot.*

1902 in medicine. It did not take him long to learn that his real function in life was to act as Holmes's biographer and general factotum. Medicine must always play a subsidiary role. Let us consider two cases in which Doctor Watson and Biographer Watson come into conflict.

The first case is *The Engineer's Thumb* which took place after Watson's marriage when he was in practice near Paddington Station. When the unfortunate Victor Hatherley arrives one morning at his surgery minus a thumb, Watson's first act is to dress the wound. He could hardly have done less. But having done so, instead of packing the patient off to his bed as any other doctor would have done, Watson bundles him into a hansom and rushes him round to Baker Street to interview Holmes. It is Holmes, not Watson, who settles the engineer on a sofa with a pillow under his head and a glass of brandy within his reach, who tells him to lie still and make himself at home, to tell his story but stop whenever he is tired. Watson makes no comment. So far as he is concerned Hatherley has ceased to be a patient and has become a character in a Sherlock Holmes case.

One would have thought that a man who had had no normal sleep the night before, had narrowly escaped being crushed to death, had been the victim of a murderous attack in which his thumb had been amputated by a butcher's cleaver, had fallen from the upper floor window of a house and had been left lying unconscious for several hours, his clothes sodden with dew and his coat-sleeve drenched with blood, might, with advantage, at this stage have retired to his bed. But no, within three hours he is in a train accompanied by Holmes, Watson, Inspector Bradstreet and a plainclothes man heading once more for Eyford, in Berkshire, the scene of the previous night's adventure, and it is not until the mystery has been finally solved that the unfortunate man is allowed to retire to a much-needed rest.

An even more remarkable example of the triumph of Watson the biographer over Watson the doctor is encountered in *The Resident Patient.* Holmes and Watson arrive at Dr. Percy Trevelyan's house to find Blessington, alias Sutton, hanging by his neck from a cord attached to a hook on the ceiling. Surely the first act of a doctor, or indeed of anyone else, would be to cut him down and to endeavour immediately to restore his respiration before it was too late. Instead the body is allowed to remain hanging whilst Holmes first questions Inspector Lanner and then examines the cigar-ends, the lock, the key, the bed, the carpet, the chairs, the mantelpiece, the body and the rope. Only after all this has been done is the body cut down.

It must of course be admitted that Holmes and Watson were not the first arrivals on the scene of the crime. The discovery was made by Dr. Percy Trevelyan, the distinguished author of a monograph upon obscure nervous lesions which had won the Bruce Pinkerton[1] medal. His failure to take any remedial action was of course even more negligent than Watson's, and a similar criticism must be made of Inspector Lanner of Scotland Yard, who had also been called in before Holmes and Watson arrived. Lanner never appears again in any subsequent case. Nor, for that matter, does the author of the monograph upon obscure

[1] In spite of considerable research we have been unable to discover any connection between this gentleman and Bruce-Partington, the inventor of the submarine.

nervous lesions. We cannot help feeling that at the inquest the coroner must have made some fairly caustic comments.

In fairness, however, to Watson it must also be recorded that he acted with much greater promptness in similar circumstances a year later in the case of *The Stockbroker's Clerk*. Realizing that Beddington had only been hanging for a few seconds, Holmes and Watson lost no time in releasing him and managed to save his life. But whereas Blessington of *The Resident Patient* was the victim of a murder who wanted very much to live, Beddington of *The Stockbroker's Clerk* had been thwarted in an attempt to commit suicide. Presumably therefore Mr. Beddington in this world and Mr. Blessington in the next are both regarding the final result with considerable dissatisfaction.

A further indication of Watson's limitations as a medical man is afforded by his failure to detect the imposture when Holmes was shamming illness in the cases of *The Reigate Squires* and *The Dying Detective*.

But whatever may have been his deficiencies as a doctor, few people could tell a story as well as Watson. He was admirably equipped to record Holmes's exploits and before long the inevitable happened. He had no intention of acting in this capacity when they first met. Holmes's occupation was unknown to him and presumably he was simply waiting until his health improved and a favourable opportunity occurred to purchase a practice. But within a few weeks Holmes had disclosed to him that he was a detective and Watson had himself assisted him in a case. Henceforward his main object was to act as Holmes's chronicler. For the time being, he abandoned his attempts to acquire a practice. After his marriage, it is true, he did make a belated start, but he was always ready the moment that Holmes's summons came to throw over his patients and return headlong to Baker Street, and there can be little doubt that this was a wise and far-sighted course.

Before long he was busily engaged in writing up innumerable cases, though six years were to elapse before the first of these, *A Study in Scarlet*, appeared in print. In *Thor Bridge* he tells us of a travel-worn and battered tin dispatch-box with the name John H. Watson, M.D., Late Indian Army, painted on the lid which is (or was) in the vaults of Cox & Co., at Charing Cross. This box is (or was) crammed full with records of unpublished cases. They were apparently for the most part rough notes, for he speaks of 'editing them.' He had no time to write a case in its final form immediately after he had dealt with it. Before he could do so he would be called away by a later case.

When it came to the final revision he had to rely on his original notes, supplemented by his memory. Sometimes these were inadequate. He would guess dates which he had omitted to note, and the guess was not always accurate. His writing was frequently indecipherable, especially his figures. His '9' resembled an '8' and his '4' could be mistaken for a '2.' His proof correction was perfunctory, to say the least of it. He could, for instance, pass a page on which a horse-race was referred to, first as 'the Wessex Cup' and later as 'the Wessex Plate.'[1]

Inaccuracies of this sort did not trouble him. Nor apparently did they trouble Holmes. His criticism was not that Watson was inaccurate, but that he romanti-

[1] *Silver Blaze.*

cized. Here for instance, is Holmes's opinion of *A Study in Scarlet*:

'Honestly, I cannot congratulate you upon it. Detection is, or ought to be, an exact science, and should be treated in the same cold and unemotional manner. You have attempted to tinge it with romanticism, which produces much the same effect as if you worked a love story or an elopement into the fifth proposition of Euclid.'[1]

Fortunately Watson completely disregarded this advice. If he had taken it we might have missed such masterpieces as *The Man with the Twisted Lip* and *The Hound of the Baskervilles*.

Did Holmes ever regret his decision to make Watson his chronicler? If so, it was in vain. Fate had decreed that they should be for ever linked together. The wheels of chance had begun to spin; the wheels of a hansom conveying these two strangely assorted companions through the fog-bound streets of Victorian London post-haste to the scene of some bizarre crime. The dispatch box which was later to find its way to the vaults of Messrs. Cox & Co. was still invitingly empty, but it would not remain empty much longer. If that box and its contents are still in existence there is a job waiting for somebody.

[1] *The Sign of Four.*

CHAPTER FIVE

The Home of Holmes

BEFORE we proceed further there is one preliminary problem for consideration, and for once it is a problem of place and not of time. Whereabouts in Baker Street was 221B?

One thing at least is certain. The building that to-day bears the number 221 never housed Sherlock Holmes. For in those days it was not in Baker Street at all, but in Upper Baker Street. In 1930 Upper Baker Street was merged in Baker Street and both were renumbered. In the account that follows we refer to the numbers as they are to-day and not as they were in Holmes's time, and we have adopted the same course where there has been a change in the name of a street.

A further objection to this building and also to No. 111 which is the selection of Dr. Gray C. Briggs of St. Louis, is that both are much too close to Baker Street Underground Station. In neither case would a passenger from the Underground take a cab to visit Holmes. He would no sooner have got into the cab than he would have to get out again. Both buildings, in fact, are much too far north to be reconciled with the evidence of either *The Empty House* or *The Beryl Coronet*.

We must admit at once that it is not possible to identify any particular house with certainty. Yet we can eliminate all but a very few. This process of elimination is in three distinct stages:

Stage 1. All available evidence points to a house on the west side of Baker Street in the block that lies between Blandford Street and Dorset Street. Any solution that ends outside this block should be rejected out of hand.

Stage 2. In this block there is a fair case for excluding all except Nos. 59, 61 and 63.

Stage 3. As between these three there is really very little to choose, and we are not justified in eliminating any of them, but if anything, the advantage is slightly in favour of No. 61.

The evidence is as follows:

STAGE I

(1) *It was South of Dorset Street.*

The source of information here is *The Beryl Coronet*. On a winter's morning in which the snow lay piled up high in the middle of the road but had been swept clear from the pavements, the unfortunate banker, Alexander Holder, hurried down Baker Street to visit Holmes. He tells us that 'I came to Baker Street by the Underground, and hurried from there on foot, for the cabs go slowly through this snow.'

It was therefore a journey for which he would normally have taken a cab, and as Dorset Street is only about 300 yards from the Underground, any shorter journey seems unlikely, even allowing for the fact that he describes himself as a man who takes very little exercise.

Further evidence to fix the northern boundary at

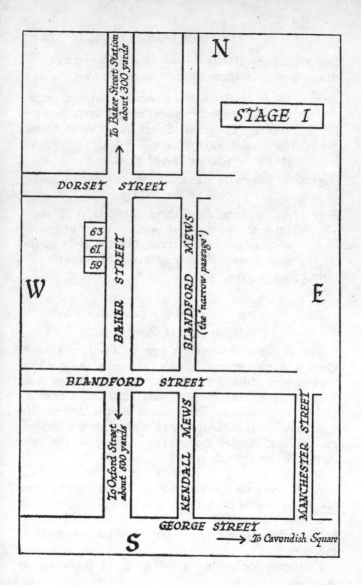

'And so down Regent Street'

Dorset Street is forthcoming in *The Empty House* which is considered later.

(2) *It was north of Blandford Street.*

Here our authority is *The Hound of the Baskervilles.* After Sir Henry Baskerville and Dr. Mortimer had left his rooms, Holmes, realizing that Sir Henry's enemy would probably be shadowing them, decided that he and Watson would adopt a similar course. But a certain amount of time was lost, as the famous dressing-gown had to be exchanged for a frock-coat and boots had to be put on, so that by the time they reached the front door 'Dr. Mortimer and Baskerville were still visible about two hundred yards ahead of us in the direction of Oxford Street.' Declining Watson's offer to run on and stop them, Holmes 'quickened his pace until we had decreased the distance which divided us by about half. Then, still keeping a hundred yards behind, we followed into Oxford Street and so down Regent Street.'

The second pair had therefore gained a hundred yards on the first pair before the first pair had reached Oxford Street. They had done this without running or without walking at such an excessive speed as to attract the attention of anyone in the street who might, in fact, be Sir Henry Baskerville's unknown enemy. The distance from Blandford Street to Oxford Street is about 500 yards and this can be taken as the minimum distance in which the requisite 100 yards gain could be established in those circumstances.

Here again, there is further evidence in *The Empty House* to fix our southern boundary at Blandford Street.

(3) *It was on the west side of Baker Street.*

This is clear beyond all possible doubt from the account given in *The Empty House* where Holmes took Watson to an empty house which was on the opposite side of Baker Street to their own home. They approached it from the east via Cavendish Square, Manchester Street and Blandford Street. From Blandford Street they turned into an unnamed 'narrow passage' which gave access to the back entrance of the empty house. It was not until he was inside the empty house and looking out of its front window that Watson realized to his astonishment that they had reached Baker Street and that 'our own old quarters' were on the opposite side of the street. Accordingly the empty house must have been on the east side and the 'old quarters' on the west.

Next, as to the identity of the 'narrow passage.' Just before Blandford Street runs into Baker Street we get two such passages, Blandford Mews on the north side, and Kendall Mews on the south. It is unlikely that they turned into the latter, for they had started from Cavendish Square which is to the south. Coming from Cavendish Square therefore they would have made an unnecessary detour when they turned into Manchester Street instead of continuing straight on into George Street. Holmes knew his London far too well to lose time and distance in that way. A man who could travel in a hansom on a foggy night from the Lyceum Theatre, via Vauxhall Bridge, to Coldharbour Lane, Brixton, and could give his companion the name of every single street through which they passed[1] would

[1] *The Sign of Four.*

surely know the shortest route in a district which was within a stone's throw of his own front door.

So Blandford Mews must be 'the narrow passage' and, if so, both buildings would be in the section of Baker Street that lies between Blandford Street and Dorset Street, the empty house being on the east side and Holmes's rooms on the west. We can now pass on to the second stage in our process of elimination.

STAGE 2

Our chief source of information is once again *The Hound of the Baskervilles*. The following points may be noted:

(1) The distance from Blandford Street to Dorset Street is about 150 yards.

(2) When Sir Henry Baskerville and his companion visited Holmes they were shadowed by Sir Henry's sinister, black-bearded opponent. Both were in cabs and they came from the direction of Oxford Street.

(3) The first cab pulled up outside Holmes's front door. The second cab stopped 'halfway down the street,' i.e. half-way between Holmes's apartments and Blandford Street.

(4) It can be assumed that there was a space of at least fifty yards between the two cabs. If the second were to get any closer to the first it ran the risk of attracting the attention of the occupants of the first cab which would be the very last thing that the black-bearded gentleman in the second cab would desire.

(5) The first cab did not stop exactly opposite to the corner of Baker Street and Dorset Street, or even at the second house from the corner. If it had done so the driver of the second cab would have been able to pinpoint it exactly; when, at a later stage, he was

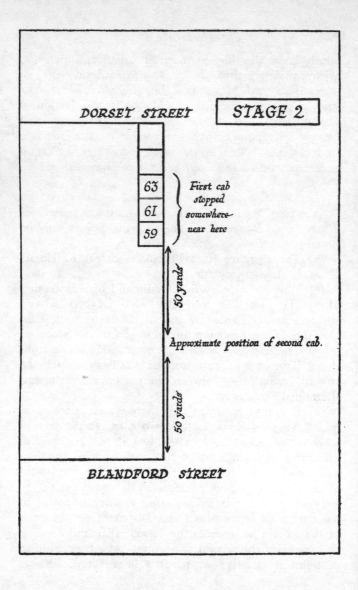

questioned by Holmes. This he was unable to do. He could only say that it was 'somewhere near here.'

A glance at the accompanying plan (*Stage* 2) will show that to fit *all* the above facts it is necessary to have a location at roughly three-quarters of the way from Blandford Street to Dorset Street, and that the issue is thus narrowed down to Nos. 59, 61 and 63.

STAGE 3

As between these three buildings there is so little to choose that we are not really justified in carrying the process of elimination any further. It might perhaps be argued however that No. 61 as the middle one of the three has the best claim.[1] A more ruthless slaughter in Stage 2 might have removed No. 59 under the third and fourth paragraphs and No. 63 under the fifth.

There we must leave it. All three are possible but we have a slight preference for 61. There were three famous occupants of this elusive building, Holmes, Watson and the faithful landlady, Mrs. Hudson. Why not, then, give one building to each? In the unlikely event of the government of London passing into our hands we propose to put up three plaques. That on No. 61 will commemorate Holmes, whilst those on No. 59 and 63 will be allocated respectively to Watson and Mrs. Hudson.

[1] By a curious coincidence No. 61 is at the present time tenanted by Messrs. Walkers and Holtzapffel Ltd., who bear the first two letters of 'Watson' and the first three of 'Holmes.' Does this mean that the ghosts of the original occupants of Baker Street have returned in a new line of business?

CHAPTER SIX

The Early Eighties

WATSON had been wounded in the battle of Maiwand which took place in July 1880. Thereafter he came to London as we have already seen, and met Holmes on a winter's afternoon. Presumably, therefore, this was in 1881 though we are not in fact told so. All that we know is that Gregson's letter which led to the events recorded in *A Study in Scarlet* arrived on March 4th. Before he mentions this letter he tells us that during 'the first week or so nobody called,' and there is also a passage which runs 'as the weeks went by.' This suggests that they first took up their residence in Baker Street about the end of January 1881.

Apart from the fact that it was Watson's first case the chief interest in *A Study in Scarlet* lies in the enthusiasm with which Scotland Yard plunged into this affair. Perhaps they wished to impress their Transatlantic brethren by demonstrating that they were quite capable of discovering the murderer of Enoch J. Drebber of Cleveland, Ohio. But whether or not Anglo-American rivalry entered into the matter, they adopted the extreme course of detailing both their leading men, Lestrade and Gregson, to take on the case. Thanks to Holmes the murderer was discovered, but apparently the authorities were not satisfied, for the experiment was never repeated. Henceforward Lestrade and Gregson went their separate ways and we never again find them both appearing in the same case.

Perhaps at this stage a word may be said about Scotland Yard and its representatives. Of these, G. Lestrade is easily the most important. We meet him in no less than twelve different cases. He was still going strong in 1902 at the time of *The Three Garridebs*, though if we can believe his own account he had already put in twenty years service prior to *A Study in Scarlet* in 1881! By the time that we say good-bye to this rat-faced little man we feel that we know him almost as well as Watson himself, and with the years our affection for him grows. Invariably he required Holmes to put him on the right track, but thereafter he could hang on with the tenacity of a bulldog, and as Holmes found on more than one occasion he was an invaluable man to have by one's side in a tight corner.

Next to Lestrade, but toiling far behind him, come the burly Tobias Gregson and young Stanley Hopkins, the rising star of the nineties, who each make four separate appearances. Of the rest, Bradstreet and the aggressive Peter Athelney Jones are encountered twice, and about a dozen others each appear once.

Poor Scotland Yard! Invariably they took the wrong turning. The only thing they seem to have learnt throughout the years was that Holmes could usually be relied on to see them through. The derisory attitude of the professional for an eccentric but somewhat lucky amateur gradually gives place to a reluctant respect and admiration. The Gregson of *The Red Circle* is a much more respectful colleague than the Gregson of *A Study in Scarlet*. Even the truculent Athelney Jones of *The Sign of Four* has mellowed considerably when we meet him again three years later in *The Red-Headed*

League. But perhaps the best example is Lestrade's spontaneous tribute after the triumphant conclusion of *The Six Napoleons.*

'I've seen you handle a good many cases, Mr. Holmes, but I don't know that I ever knew a more workmanlike one than that. We're not jealous of you at Scotland Yard. No, Sir, we are very proud of you, and if you come down to-morrow there's not a man, from the oldest inspector to the youngest constable, who would not be glad to shake you by the hand.'

But if they learnt to appreciate Holmes at his true value, they learnt nothing else. In 1903 when Holmes retired they had no more ideas on the detection of criminals than they had when he first came to their notice in 1878. In spite of his good advice they completely failed to study his methods, and the depressing conclusion must be drawn that after 1903 the number of undetected criminals at large in London and elsewhere must have increased very considerably.

To return once more to Watson, *A Study in Scarlet* opened his eyes to a brave new world. Whilst waiting for his health to improve and for a lucrative practice to appear on the horizon, he decided that he would write an account of the case in which he had recently taken part. This he proceeded to do in a leisurely manner throughout the year 1881, and during that year he took very little part, if any, in Holmes's activities.

Since he himself does not anywhere record that 1881 was passed in this manner, it is incumbent on us to produce the evidence. This we submit is the clear implication of the opening paragraph of *The Five Orange Pips.*

'When I glance over my notes and records of the

Sherlock Holmes cases between the years '82 and '90, I am faced by so many which present strange and interesting features.'

Why is '81 omitted? Clearly because *A Study in Scarlet* was the only case in that year of which he had any record. After this case it was no longer necessary for him to make a discreet withdrawal to his bedroom when a client arrived to see Holmes, as had been his custom during the first few weeks. From *The Yellow Face*, which took place in the following year, we learn that by that time he had been present at many such interviews. But he probably took no further part in the proceedings and, above all, he kept no notes. The idea of a permanent partnership had not yet occurred to either man.

By the end of the year he had finished his narrative entitled *A Study in Scarlet* and had shown it to Holmes. In spite of later criticisms[1] Holmes was sufficiently impressed to suggest (or to agree to the suggestion) that henceforward Watson should keep a record of his more interesting and important cases. From that time onward he was Holmes's authorized chronicler, though it was not till 1887 that *A Study in Scarlet*, the first-born, was published.

In March 1882 the episode of *The Yellow Face* occurred. As with so many of the early cases, Watson gives the season, but leaves it to us to supply the year. The indications are that this is a very early case. We are told that Holmes seldom took exercise just for its own sake, but one day in the early spring he had so far relaxed as to go for a walk with Watson in the Park, where the first faint shoots of green were breaking out upon the elms. It was nearly five by the time they got

[1] *The Sign of Four.*

back to find that they had missed a new client. Tired of waiting, he had departed, leaving only a pipe behind him. The pipe of course was quite sufficient for Holmes to make a fairly adequate reconstruction. But a reconstructed client was still an absent one, and as Holmes remarked reproachfully to Watson: 'So much for afternoon walks!'

Apparently this was the first occasion on which they had ever played truant. All through the year 1881 Holmes had stayed at home when not actually engaged on a case, lest he should miss a prospective client. It would be asking too much to expect him to go through a second year confined to his quarters, to hold out for two whole years from January 1881 to March 1883. We can safely assume that he succumbed on the first tempting spring afternoon of 1882.

Further evidence that this is a very early case is contained in Holmes's exclamation: 'I was badly in need of a case.' There had been a slump. He was not yet fully established. Soon his reputation would be such that idle periods when clients were scarce would be a thing of the past.

He had known cases go wrong before he came to Baker Street, but probably this was the first instance of a failure since his association with Watson had started. Hence his concluding remark to him: 'If it should ever strike you that I am getting a little over-confident in my powers, or giving less pains to a case than it deserves, kindly whisper "Norbury" in my ear, and I shall be infinitely obliged to you.'

In the summer of the same year followed the case of *The Greek Interpreter*. Here again we are told the season but have to deduce the year. It is here, for the first time, that we meet Sherlock's elder brother, Mycroft, a sort of nationalized version of Sherlock, his equal in observation and deduction, but without energy or ambition. He could not be bothered to verify his own solutions, and would rather be considered wrong than go to the trouble of proving himself right. He could solve a problem, but was quite incapable of working out the practical points which were necessary before it could be submitted to a judge and jury.

Clearly therefore there was only one thing that could be done with such a person. He must be put in complete control of the British Government. In fact, as Sherlock put it, 'you might in one sense say he *is* the British Government.' At the very centre of the Whitehall labyrinth was Mycroft, controlling and directing everything. 'The conclusions of every department are passed to him, and he is the central exchange, the clearing house which makes out the balance. All other men are specialists, but his specialism is omniscience. We will suppose that a Minister needs information as to a point which involves the Navy, India, Canada and the bimetallic question; he could get his separate advices from various departments upon each, but only Mycroft can focus them all, and say off-hand how each factor would affect the other. . . . Again and again his word has decided the national policy.'[1]

Mycroft Holmes would seem to have been born too soon. Had he lived about fifty years later he would have found a more suitable world for his particular talents.

Now Mycroft's peculiar role in British politics was not disclosed to Watson at the time of *The Greek Interpreter*. On that occasion he was merely introduced as one who audited the books of some of the Govern-

[1] *The Bruce-Partington Plans.*

ment departments. Sherlock waited until the case of
The Bruce-Partington Plans which took place in the third
week of November 1895, before letting Watson into the
secret. By 1895 Watson had only a vague recollection
of *The Greek Interpreter* which at once suggests that
there must be a very long interval between the two
incidents.

As to the reason for this secrecy Sherlock's explanation is: 'I did not know you quite so well in those days.
One has to be discreet when one talks about high
matters of state.' This we think justifies us in placing
this case as early as 1882. By that time they had lived
together for about eighteen months. If by the end of the
first two years Holmes had still felt doubts about his
companion, he would probably have made arrange-
ments to terminate their association and would have
left Baker Street. By the time the case of *Chorles
Augustus Milverton* occurred Holmes had acquired such
complete confidence in Watson's discretion that he was
able to show him a photograph in a shop window of a
woman who had been seen by both of them to commit
a murder, and the name on the photograph was that of
the wife of a great nobleman and statesman. This, as
we shall presently demonstrate, was in the month of
January 1883.

A third reason why this case can hardly be later than
the summer of 1882 is to be found in the opening
sentence: 'During my long and intimate acquaintance
with Mr. Sherlock Holmes I had never heard him
refer to his relations, and hardly ever to his own early
life.' Eighteen months is indeed a long time to live with
a man in ignorance of the fact that he has a brother.
To extend this period by another year is out of the
question, unless Holmes had some reason for concealing

his brother, and in that event he would never have produced him at all.

Against these three reasons for putting the case as early as the summer of 1882 must be set Mycroft's remark to Watson. 'I hear of Sherlock everywhere since you became his chronicler.' Since the first publication, *A Study in Scarlet*, was in December 1887, it follows that this remark can not have been made before 1888 at the very earliest. But by that time Watson was married and living away from Baker Street, which is clearly not the case in *The Greek Interpreter*.

The most probable explanation is that it was not Mycroft at all who paid Watson this compliment, but a client of Holmes at a much earlier date. Watson was flattered and wished to have some permanent record of this tribute to the part which he had played in building up Holmes's reputation. Unfortunately however, this client had consulted Holmes about a particularly dull, uninteresting case which Watson had no possible excuse for narrating. Accordingly he transferred the incident to the case which he was at that time writing up from his notes, which happened to be *The Greek Interpreter*. We cannot find it in our hearts to blame him.

The next two cases with which we are concerned have not previously been bracketed, but can be dealt with simultaneously as they have several points in common. They are *Charles Augustus Milverton* and *The Speckled Band*. In each we have a lady in distress, terrorized by a sinister scoundrel; in each there is a more-or-less unlawful entry by Holmes and Watson into the villain's home and in each an exciting night comes to a climax in the violent and unexpected death of the villain.

Milverton presents us with much the same sort of problem as *The Yellow Face* and *The Greek Interpreter*. Watson is apparently unmarried and living in Baker Street. But the choice here is even wider than in those two cases. For they were both published in 1893 and must therefore relate to the period before the first marriage, but *Milverton* was not published until 1904 and therefore could have taken place after the marriage had ended. The only information available is, as usual, the season. This time it is winter.

The Speckled Band by contrast is straightforward. The affair occurred in April 1883, one of the very few undisputed dates of the early period.

Now let us consider in each case the scene that occurred when it was decided to invade the enemy's camp. In *The Speckled Band* Holmes is almost non-chalant when he suggests that they should spend the night in Dr. Grimesby Roylott's house at Stoke Moran, Surrey.

'Do you know, Watson, I have really some scruples as to taking you to-night. There is a distinct element of danger.'

'Can I be of assistance?'

'Your presence might be invaluable.'

'Then I shall certainly come.'

'It is very kind of you.'

There, without any further fuss, the matter ends. Compare this with the palaver that occurs when a similar decision is made to burgle Charles Milverton's home, Appledore Towers, Hampstead. It takes over two pages to describe. Watson is appalled at the idea and begs Holmes to think what he is doing. A long argument follows. Holmes is still determined to go. Then Watson announces that he is coming too. It is now Holmes's turn to protest, but Watson sticks to his guns and threatens to give Holmes away to the police unless he is allowed to accompany him. 'You cannot help me,' says Holmes. (Compare this with 'Your presence might be invaluable.') Finally it is decided that both will go, and with the excitement and enthusiasm of two men about to carry out their first burglary they plunge into an animated conversation on the technicalities of nickel-plated jemmies, diamond-tipped glass cutters, adaptable keys, rubber-soled shoes and black silk masks.

After all, what were the relative risks of the two enterprises? Let us investigate the two home teams. At Appledore Towers there was Charles Augustus Milverton who looked like Mr. Pickwick, but (unlike Mr. Winkle) knew how to handle a gun. There was a rather fearsome dog, but Holmes, with memories perhaps of the dog in his college days, had had the foresight to disguise as a workman and to become engaged to Milverton's housemaid, Agatha, with the result that this young lady, for obvious reasons, took care that the animal was locked up at an early hour. In addition, Milverton's establishment was liberally stocked with faithful secretaries, housemaids and under-gardeners.

The Stoke Moran contingent is headed by Dr. Grimesby Roylott, complete with black top-hat, frock-coat, high gaiters and a hunting-crop. His hat brushed the crossbar of the doorway, so he can hardly have been under six-foot-six. His large face was seared with a thousand wrinkles, burned yellow by the sun and marked with every evil passion, whilst his deep-set bile-shot eyes and high, thin, fleshless nose made him look like a bird of prey. He possessed a cheetah which had a disconcerting habit of whining in the garden at night. Next on the list was a baboon resembling a hideous and distorted child, also a nocturnal habitué of the garden. Last but not least there was the deadly 'speckled band' itself.

Would any reasonable burglar hesitate between the two? Give him every time the known horrors of Hampstead rather than the Stoke Moran Zoo!

Why then did Holmes and Watson make so much more heavy weather of Hampstead than of Stoke Moran? Obviously because Hampstead was their first exploit of this sort and having got through it safely they subsequently went into Stoke Moran with the confidence of the experienced.

This means that the Milverton episode took place before April 1883. But it can hardly be earlier than the winter which had just come to an end, for Holmes says: 'We have shared the same room for some years.' At that time they had in fact shared it for approximately two years, a period which would scarcely qualify for the description 'some years' in ordinary parlance. Still Watson's ideas of time were always rather vague and the probability is that he misquoted Holmes who in fact used the phrase 'for some time.'

At this stage it may be convenient to consider the argument of Mr. Bell who maintains that the correct date of the Milverton case is February 1884. First, he holds that it happened in the early years when they were still young enough to scramble over a six foot wall and run two miles across Hampstead Heath without stopping, though they were wearing dress-clothes and overcoats. Whilst we agree that they were in fact young men at the time, we very much doubt whether the two miles non-stop run ever took place.

'His deep-set, bile-shot eyes and high, thin, fleshless nose
made him look like a bird of prey'

For apparently they were not pursued out of the garden and although a man might run for a quarter of a mile before he realized that he was not being followed, a two-mile run in these circumstances would be fantastic. Writing the case up many years later, Watson's memory probably played him tricks which led to this exaggeration.

Because of the expression 'for some years' he considers that 1883 is too early and by a process of elimination he arrives at February 1884. We can only repeat that we cannot believe that two people who had handled *The Speckled Band* so successfully in April 1883 could make such a fuss before trying conclusions with Milverton ten months later.

Mr. Bell's method of ascertaining the month, which must be either December, January or February, can now be considered. He begins by excluding the month of December in every year on the grounds that few marriages take place in Advent. It will be recalled that the Earl of Dovercourt and Lady Eva Brackwell were to have been married on the 18th of the month, and the 18th of December falls in Advent. Here again we must join issue. An investigation of the marriage notices in *The Times* during this period discloses that many marriages did take place during Advent. They may possibly be slightly fewer than in the months of January and February, but the decrease is certainly not apparent. There is no justification whatsoever for assuming that either the Earl or his fiancée were particularly orthodox in religious observance. The month of December cannot be excluded on these or any other grounds.

With the rest of Mr. Bell's argument we are in complete agreement. He points out that the month must be one in which the 13th, 14th and 18th are all weekdays. This is deduced as follows:

The 13th. Milverton told Holmes that if the money were not paid on the 14th there would be no wedding on the 18th. On the day they decided to burgle Milverton, Holmes said that the next day was the last day of grace. The burglary therefore was carried out on the night of the 13th which must have been a weekday, for Holmes and Watson put on their dress-clothes so that they might appear to be theatre-goers homeward bound.

The 14th. On the morning following the burglary Holmes took Watson to a shop in Oxford Street and showed him a photograph of the lady they had seen on the previous night. This could not have happened on a Sunday, for in Victorian times the blinds would have been drawn.

The 18th. This was the day of the wedding.

We have already given our reasons for maintaining that the case happened in the winter 1882–83. All that now remains is to apply the above test to the three months concerned. When we do so January and February are both eliminated. It was in December 1882 therefore, that the event occurred which will be for ever memorable in the history of Hampstead.

CHAPTER SEVEN

Snow and Stains

NONE of the sixty cases actually reported by Watson or Holmes appear to fall in the years 1884 and 1885. But probably some of those which are only mentioned incidentally are to be located in these years. These cases of which we obtain such a tantalizingly brief glimpse must be as numerous as those which are recorded. Most of them appear in solitary state, but here and there we get a string of them.

One such series appears in *The Five Orange Pips* and purports to be a list of the cases which took place in 1887. These apparently included the adventure of the Paradol Chamber, of the Amateur Mendicant Society, of the barque *Sophy Anderson*, of the Grice Patersons in the island of Uffa and of the Camberwell poisoning case where Holmes was able, by winding up the dead man's watch to prove that it had been wound up two hours ago. Watson expresses the hope that some of these 1887 cases will appear in print at a later date. But it was not to be. All five were lost to posterity. Four cases were subsequently published which occurred in 1887, but they were four different cases.

It seems highly unlikely that anyone could change his views as to what were, and what were not important cases so quickly. At the time of writing *The Five Orange Pips* he thinks of the year 1887 and recalls five cases, but within a year or two all five have faded from his

mind to be replaced by four others. The explanation
must surely be that he made a mistake and that the
five cases relate to some other year. If so, it must be a
year in which there are few if any reported cases, or
we are faced again with the same difficulty. Obviously,
then, 1884 or 1885 is the year. Probably Watson put
his rough notes of these five cases into the same folder
or envelope. He knew at once that they all belonged to
the same year, but his memory played him false when
he ascribed them to 1887. Later, apparently, he began
to have doubts and he decided to withhold publication
until he was certain of the correct year. But certainty
was never achieved. Meanwhile new cases were con-
stantly appearing to occupy his attention. So the record
of the years 1884–85 was never written, and the world
is the poorer, for it would like to have known what
exactly happened to the Grice Patersons on the island
of Uffa, and what were the objects, constitution, and
history of the Amateur Mendicant Society.

Before we leave '85 there is one further comment to be
made. If the story previously recorded[1] of that preposterous old humbug, the elder Trevor were to be
taken at its face value, this would be the year of *The
'Gloria Scott'* and Holmes would still be an undergraduate at Oxford!

In 1886 we come to that exceedingly cold affair,
The Beryl Coronet. There is snow everywhere; snow
heaped up in the centre of Baker Street causes the
harassed Alexander Holder to walk instead of taking a
cab. Snow in the suburbs offers a god-sent opportunity
for one-legged men (and others) to leave their tracks
all over Streatham. Wherever we look there is snow.

The case apparently started on a February morning

[1] See page 30.

before Watson's marriage, whilst he was still living in Baker Street. Whether he was married in 1887 or 1888 is a matter of acute controversy which will be considered at a later stage. For our present purposes let us assume that the later date is correct, as it will give us a wider choice. In what years prior to 1889 was there snow on the ground in February?

The year 1881 would suit our purpose admirably for there were two heavy falls, but, unhappily, this is too early, for *A Study in Scarlet* which is obviously the first Baker Street case reported by Watson started on March 4th. From 1882 to 1888, with one exception, there was either no snow at all or insufficient to cover the ground. Nor do the last two or three days in January of those years yield any better result.

The one exception is February 28, 1886. Snow fell during the day for several hours leaving a substantial covering on the ground before night. This then must be the night on which the attempt was made to steal the coronet. But Watson is wrong when he says that it was a February morning when he looked out of the window and saw Alexander Holder coming down the street. This happened on the next day, March 1st.

This case suggests that the highest social and financial circles conducted their affairs with extreme levity. For we find that one whose 'name is a household word all over the earth,—one of the highest, noblest, most exalted names in England' being temporarily embarrassed, had pawned the Beryl Coronet, 'one of the most precious public possessions of the Empire,' to raise a loan of fifty thousand pounds. Further, the senior partner of 'the second largest private banking concern in the City of London,' instead of at once locking it up in his safe, had proceeded to carry it blithely home to Streatham with him without even taking the elementary precaution of keeping its whereabouts overnight a secret. Surely this was inviting the trouble that subsequently occurred.

The same distressing irresponsibility in high circles is apparent in our next case, *The Second Stain*, though this time it is in the political world—British and foreign. Here we encounter a foreign potentate who, ruffled by some recent colonial developments, had written without the knowledge of his ministers a most provocative letter, the publication of which would have undoubtedly involved the country in a major war. Common sense suggests that the best course would have been to put the offending document straight into the fire. But the Government thought otherwise. It went into the Foreign Secretary's dispatch-box and back to his home where it was as safe and secure as the Beryl Coronet was in Streatham.

Two problems face us with *The Second Stain*, for in addition to ascertaining the date some explanation appears to be required as to why there are apparently three separate cases all referred to as 'the second stain.'

The earliest reference is in *The Yellow Face* which was first published in February 1893, and is as follows:

'Now and again, however, it chanced that even when he erred the truth was still discovered. I have notes of some half-dozen cases of the kind, of which the affair of 'the second stain,' and that which I am now about to recount are the two which present the strangest features of interest.'

Eight months later, in October 1893 we get a further reference to a 'second stain' which on this occasion comes from *The Naval Treaty*.

'The July which immediately succeeded my marriage

was made memorable by three cases of interest in
which I had the privilege of being associated with
Sherlock Holmes and of studying his methods. I find
them recorded in my notes under the headings of
'The Adventure of the Second Stain,' 'The Adventure
of the Naval Treaty,' and 'The Adventure of the Tired
Captain.' The first of these, however, deals with
interests of such importance and implicates so many of
the first families in the kingdom that for many years
it will be impossible to make it public. No case, however, in which Holmes was ever engaged has illustrated
the value of his analytical methods so clearly or has
impressed those who were associated with him so
deeply. I still retain an almost verbatim report of the
interview in which he demonstrated the true facts of
the case to Monsieur Dubuque, of the Paris police,
and Fritz von Waldbaum, the well-known specialist
of Danzig, both of whom had wasted their energies
upon what proved to be side-issues. The new century
will have come, however, before the story can be
safely told. Meanwhile I pass on to the second upon
my list . . .'

Brief as is the first of these extracts, it will be seen
that it conflicts with the second, for in the one he fails
to obtain a solution, but in the other he not only solves
the mystery, but triumphs over his Continental
colleagues. It would appear therefore that these are
two different cases.

The last of the three 'second stains' is the account of
this case which was first published in 1904. This
conflicts with the first account, for Holmes was successful. Nor does it really bear much resemblance to the
second. It did not 'implicate so many of the first
families of the kingdom.' Dubuque, of the Paris police,

and von Waldbaum, of the Danzig police were both conspicuous by their absence. Danzig, indeed, played no part in the affair at all. It is true that the Paris police were consulted in connection with the murder of Eduardo Lucas. But the information that they gave was both accurate and helpful. On the main problem, the whereabouts of the missing letter, they were not consulted at all. How could they be, when the Cabinet had kept its loss a secret from everyone except Holmes and Watson. It would appear therefore that this is a third case differing from the other two.

Are we then to assume that there are three separate cases all bearing the same name? That Holmes had three cases all relating to two stains is in the highest degree improbable. But coincidence is stretched even further, for in each case the second stain is in some way significant and different from the first. If it were not, then the case would simply be called 'The Two Stains,' just as we have 'The Five Orange Pips' and *not* 'The Fifth Orange Pip.' Moreover, if by some incredible fluke there really were three such cases, Watson could not fail to have realized the coincidence, and he would make some attempt to distinguish them. He might, for instance, refer to them as 'The First Second Stain,' 'The Second Second Stain,' and 'The Third Second Stain.' Instead he is apparently quite oblivious of the difficulty, and writes the whole time as if there were only one single case.

Beyond all further argument, the only conclusion consistent with sanity is that there *is* only one 'second stain,' and that the two earlier references are fictitious. How then do we account for them? There is, we suggest, only one possible explanation. They were messages in code. The words 'second stain' constitute a key-word warning the initiated reader that what follows, or immediately precedes, is not to be taken at its face value but is in fact a coded message. There never was such a case as 'The Tired Captain.' Dubuque and von Waldbaum never existed. The existence of the cities of Paris and Danzig is not disputed, but here they are probably being used as code symbols.

Both the messages were published in the year 1893 and, as we shall see, in that year a reason existed for sending messages in code. To forestall disappointment we would admit that we are not able to decode the messages, though the subject to which they relate, the sender and the recipient can be ascertained. But we are still dealing with the year 1886, and accordingly, it will be convenient to allow the matter to stand over until we come to 1893.

Our second problem is to find a date for the case. All that we know is that it is autumnal. All previous investigators have decided in favour of 1894. It will be recalled that the three years 1891–93 form a gap owing to Holmes's absence from Baker Street, and this gap can be extended back so far as this particular case is concerned to take in the period when Watson was married, and no longer living in Baker Street. This means that no autumn is available between 1888 and 1893.

It has been suggested that the foreign potentate who sent the ill-advised letter must be Kaiser Wilhelm II, and that as he did not come to the throne until 1888 the earliest possible date is 1894.

But this can only be so if there are three 'second stains.' If there is only one, then it must have taken place before February 1893 which, as we have seen, is the date of publication of the first of the three in *The*

Yellow Face. Any other explanation credits Watson with power to foresee the future. Unless the preposterous theory is maintained that there are three separate cases, it is clear that the autumn of 1890 must be the latest possible date.

The Kaiser has much to answer for, but in this case he must be acquitted. The 'foreign potentate' is either someone else, or he may be an invention of Watson's for the purpose of obscuring the issue. For the good doctor tells us plainly that he is giving a carefully guarded account of the incident, and that he is being deliberately vague in certain details.

Even if the theory of three separate cases is maintained there remain three further arguments in favour of the eighties and against the nineties. The first and least important is to be found in Watson's statement that Holmes was reluctant for the case to be published, but that 'I at last succeeded in obtaining his consent that a carefully guarded account of the incident should at last be laid before the public.' The repetition of the words 'at last' suggests that a long interval had elapsed, and point to the conclusion that the case was an early one.

Next we have the argument of the three spies. At the time of *The Second Stain* London contained three international spies, Oberstein, La Rothiere, and Eduardo Lucas, of whom the last named was murdered during the course of the case. At the time of *The Bruce-Partington Plans*, i.e. in November 1895, there were again three spies, Oberstein, La Rothiere, and Adolph Meyer. This time Oberstein was the unfortunate man. He went to prison for fifteen years. This means that *The Second Stain* is the earlier of the two cases, for Oberstein would hardly be able to set up as a spy again on his release from prison, and even if he did, he would not be out until 1907 at the earliest, by which time Holmes had retired.

Those, therefore, who think that the case took place in the nineties are restricted to 1894 and 1895. But here they are faced with a difficulty, for the Holmes of *The Second Stain* can rattle off the names of the spies and has all the requisite information at his fingers' ends, on the other hand, the Holmes of *The Bruce-Partington Plans* lacks this information, and has to obtain it from Mycroft. They are, accordingly, forced to cling in desperation to 1894, for it would be manifestly ridiculous to assert that he knew the spy position in September or October, but *not* in November of the same year. The year 1895 must therefore be jettisoned. at all costs, but is 1894 much better? This implies that Holmes, a man of superb memory had forgotten this important information in the course of a single year. On the other hand, if 1886 be accepted as the year of *The Second Stain*, instead of a single year we have an interval of nine years, during three of which Holmes has been out of the country. In 1886 we can infer that he had the information as the result of his investigation of earlier cases. Since then, it can be assumed, relatively few cases involving espionage had come his way. In these circumstances it would not be unreasonable to obtain Mycroft's assistance.

The last argument in favour of an earlier date is the reference to Lord Bellinger as 'twice Premier of Britain.' In 1894 the Prime Minister was Lord Rosebery, who only held that honour once. After that year one has to come right down to 1924 before one finds a man holding the office of Prime Minister for the second time. By contrast that was the situation in every single autumn throughout the 'eighties except 1885, Mr. Gladstone being Premier for the second time from 1880 to June 1885, and Lord Salisbury being Premier for the first time in 1885 and for the second time from 1886 to 1892.

To decide between the two is no easy matter. Lord Bellinger is described as 'austere, high-nosed, eagle-eyed, and dominant.' This sounds far more like a description of the Grand Old Man than of Lord Salisbury, but for this very reason we think we must choose the latter. For let us not forget Watson's statement that in certain details he is being deliberately vague. He has undoubtedly disguised Trelawney Hope, his Foreign Secretary, who is described as a young man. No Foreign Secretary throughout that period was a young man. If he intends to disguise his Foreign Secretary he will also disguise his Prime Minister. The above pen-picture can hardly be described as a disguise of Gladstone.

We think therefore that the case occurred during Lord Salisbury's second period from 1886 to 1892, and must have occurred in the autumn of a year when the offices of Prime Minister and Foreign Secretary were held by two different men. But only the first year, 1886, meets this requirement. For Lord Iddesleigh, the first Foreign Secretary, died in January 1887, and thereafter Lord Salisbury acted in both capacities. We can therefore decide that the case of *The Second Stain* took place in the autumn of 1886.

CHAPTER EIGHT

My Dear Miss Morstan

AFTER our long journey through the complications of
The Second Stain it is a relief to come to a few straightforward cases. Early in 1887 occurred the colossal
schemes of the most accomplished swindler in Europe,
Baron Maupertuis, involving the Netherland-Sumatra
Company. But though from our standpoint this case
presents no difficulty, Holmes was in a less fortunate
position, for the immense exertions occasioned by it
led to a breakdown in his health. Watson decided
that a week in the country in the month of April
would be beneficial, and took him down to Reigate.
By a fortunate chance they arrived just in time to
participate in the affair of *The Reigate Squires*. Apparently
the proposed week was reduced to three days at the
end of which they were back in London. The solution
of the mystery had proved a more effective cure than
any amount of country air.

In 1887 a terrible murderer, Bert Stevens, appealed
to Holmes to get him off.[1] Our information in this case
is restricted to the fact that Mr. Stevens was a mild-
mannered Sunday school young man. So the only
possible comment appears to be that one cannot judge
by appearances.

With the next case, *The Sign of Four*, we come for
the first time into the orbit of Watson's forthcoming

[1] *The Norwood Builder.*

marriage. Hitherto we have had to deal with a series of cases, most of which were undated, in the period prior to the marriage. There are still one or two more of these to be considered, but we are now in a period in which, in the words of Sir Desmond MacCarthy,[1] he uses the marriage as a sort of B.C. and A.D. with which to date the cases. Both the month and the year of the marriage are matters of acute controversy. Other problems, too, arise in connection with this marriage which we propose to deal with in a later chapter. Here all that we need say is that we believe that it took place at the end of November 1887, and that the ostensible dates of *The Sign of Four, The Five Orange Pips*, and *A Scandal in Bohemia* must all be revised. This may sound rather drastic, but it must be pointed out that whatever date is postulated for the marriage some revision becomes necessary.

Accordingly, we suggest that *The Sign of Four* took place, not as would appear at first sight in 1888, but in 1887. This case produced a charming lady, Miss Mary Morstan, who before the year ended had become Mrs. Watson. The letter which she had received in the morning on which she called was dated July 7th. Later in his account Watson says that it was a September evening. Probably he was misled by the 'dense drizzly fog that lay low upon the great city,' admittedly an unusual phenomenon in July. But July it must be, for it is referred to in *The Cardboard Box*, which happened during an August heatwave at a time when Watson was still unmarried.

Three more of the cases reported by Watson occurred in this period after he had met Miss Morstan, but before he had married her, two of which, *Silver Blaze*

[1] Article in *The Listener*, December 11, 1929.

and *The Noble Bachelor* overlap slightly in time, and by a curious coincidence two members of the peerage, the Duke of Balmoral and Lord Backwater played a minor part in each case.

It is evident that *The Noble Bachelor* took place in 1887, for Lord St. Simon who was born in 1846 was aged forty-one at that time. The wedding took place on October 4th, which was a Tuesday, and was reported in various papers on the 5th. On Thursday, the 6th, a single newspaper obtained a scoop by announcing the disappearance of the bride, and Holmes who was consulted on the afternoon of Friday the 7th, succeeded in solving the mystery within a few hours.

Silver Blaze, at first, seems to contain no clue as to its date beyond the fact that it is prior to Watson's marriage. But the racehorse, after whom the case is named, was 'from the Isonomy stock' and 'in his fifth year.' Isonomy first went to the stud in 1881 and accordingly 1887 is the earliest, and the only possible, year prior to his marriage.

It is an autumn case for there are two references to the fading ferns. Holmes and Watson travelled down to Tavistock on a Thursday and the race took place on the following Tuesday. In 1887 Thursday falls on September 22nd and 29th and on October 6th and 13th.

Of these September 22nd is too early, for the bracken would hardly be fading by that date. Equally October 13th is too late, for it was evening by the time they reached Tavistock, but before dark a long agenda had been completed, comprising a drive out to Colonel Ross's headquarters at King's Pyland which was apparently some distance from Tavistock, a long and very detailed investigation at King's Pyland, a journey to the scene of the crime and a further investigation, a further journey to the rival racing establishment at Capelton, and finally an interview between Holmes and Silas Brown, the Capelton trainer which lasted for quite twenty minutes. All this took place before 'the reds had all faded into greys.' If it was already evening when they first arrived in Tavistock an earlier date than October 13th is obviously essential.

How about Thursday, October 6th? If so, they left Tavistock by the midnight train and would be in London in the early morning, having been on the move for most of the previous twenty-four hours in which they had made a return journey to Devonshire and had had, in all probability, very little sleep. In these circumstances Friday might well be a day of rest. We should not expect Holmes, who rarely took exercise for its own sake[1] to go for a walk, and if Watson chose to take an easy day it would probably be for the reasons which we have just mentioned, and not for quite different reasons. But here is the situation at 3 o'clock on Friday, October 7th, as recorded *not* in *Silver Blaze* but in *The Noble Bachelor*.

'. . . he (Holmes) came home from an afternoon stroll to find a letter on the table waiting for him. I had remained indoors all day, for the weather had taken a sudden turn to rain with high autumnal winds, and the jezail bullet which I had brought back in one of my limbs as a relic of my Afghan campaign throbbed with dull persistency. With my body in one easy chair and my legs upon another, I had surrounded myself with a cloud of newspapers, until at last, saturated with the news of the day, I tossed them all aside . . .'

[1] *The Yellow Face.*

'A broad-brimmed hat, tilted in a coquettish Duchess-of-Devonshire fashion over her ear'

This does not seem the right sort of Friday to follow the Tavistock pilgrimage and we are, accordingly, left with only Thursday, September 29th. This then must be the required date, which means that the two cases overlap, and that the Wessex Cup (or Plate) was run on Tuesday, October 4th, the day of Lord St. Simon's marriage. This may have been somewhat inconvenient for Lord Backwater and for the Duke of Balmoral, whose horses, Desborough and Iris, finished second and third respectively, to Silver Blaze. We do not know for certain whether either of them saw the race. Lord Backwater was at the wedding and at the subsequent breakfast. If this was held sufficiently early in the day he might have been able to catch a fast train down to Winchester and have arrived in time to see the Wessex Cup. The defeat of Iris must have been a severe blow to the ducal finances, for he had already been compelled to sell his pictures. The Duke certainly ought to have attended his own son's wedding but rather surprisingly his name is not mentioned in the newspaper report. Needless to say, the Duchess was there. Perhaps the Duke thought that he might not have time to get in both events in the same day and decided in favour of the race. Probably it was a wise decision.

Later in that same eventful October occurred the episode of *The Resident Patient*, the last case prior to Watson's marriage. It had been a 'close, rainy day in October' and presumably fairly late in the month, for 'the first dim glimmer of daylight' only came at half-past seven in the morning. The Worthingdon bank gang were sentenced to fifteen years apiece in 1875, but did not complete their sentences. A remission of three years seems fair and reasonable, erring neither on the side of harshness nor leniency. Add twelve years to 1875 and we get 1887 which will be the year in which this case occurred.

Watson's marriage took place a few weeks after Lord St. Simon's, probably at the end of November. At all events there would seem to have been singularly little preparation for a wedding during the month of October. Was Holmes the best man? It seems unlikely or Watson would have recorded the fact. But it is possible, for he had a great respect for the first Mrs. Watson whom he described as one of the most charming young ladies whom he had ever met. He even seems to have contemplated employing her as a sort of female Watson, had not matrimony claimed her.[1] As for Watson himself, he may have imagined that his career at Baker Street had come to an end, but if so, he was soon to find that Baker Street could not be shaken off quite so easily.

[1] *The Sign of Four.*

CHAPTER NINE

My Dear Mrs. Watson

IN March 1888 the Watsons settled in Paddington, where a practice had been purchased from an elderly gentleman, named Farquhar, who was unfortunately afflicted with St. Vitus' dance. It would seem that both Dr. Farquhar and his practice were rapidly falling to pieces for, as Watson sagely observes, the public looks askance at the curative powers of the man whose own case is beyond the cure of his drugs.

For three months the practice kept him busy and he saw little of his old friend. Then one Saturday morning in June, Sherlock Holmes appeared at the surgery and before Watson realized what was happening he was in the train on the way to Birmingham to investigate the question of *The Stockbroker's Clerk*. From then onwards his real vocation was to act as Holmes's recorder. Some pretence was kept up that the practice was a going concern, but the truth slips out in *The Red-Headed League*. 'I have nothing to do to-day. My practice is never very absorbing.' Whenever Holmes required his services the practice could always be passed over to Jackson or Anstruther or the nameless 'accommodating neighbour.' Fortunately Watson's wife was an admirably sensible person who realized where destiny was leading him and raised no difficulties. His frequent absences from home must have been somewhat trying but she never complained. He tells us about his 'accom-

modating neighbour.'[1] He might well have also mentioned his 'accommodating wife.'

Our next recorded case is *The Naval Treaty* in 'the
July which immediately succeeded my marriage' and
therefore in 1888. Less than two years had elapsed since
The Second Stain and already another important document on which the security of our country might well
have depended, had gone astray. Those careless
Victorians!

In the same year followed *The Crooked Man*, which
started 'one summer night, a few months after my
marriage.' We can reasonably infer that Barclay was
married in 1857 during the Indian Mutiny, and if so,
the phrase 'upwards of thirty years' and 'this thirty
years' supply further evidence that the case occurred in
1888. We do not know the month for certain but from
the preliminary conversation on each occasion we
gather that there was a short interval between each of
the four recorded cases that took place during that
year. The other three happened respectively during the
months of June, July and September, leaving August
available for *The Crooked Man*.

The September case is *The Five Orange Pips*. At first
sight the year appears to be 1887, but this will not do,
for it occurred after the marriage. 'My wife was on a
visit to her aunt's, and for a few days I was a dweller
once more in my old quarters at Baker Street.' A later
year is accordingly required. The year 1890, however,
would be too late, for Watson, writing about the case
in November 1891 would hardly go so far astray as to
say that it happened in 1887 if it had in fact happened
as recently as September 1890. Nor can it be 1889, for
as we shall see in the next chapter, that year comprises

[1] *The Final Problem.*

a closed list of seven cases and no vacancies are available. We are therefore left with September 1888 as the date of *The Five Orange Pips*. John Openshaw, the client in this case, has the melancholy distinction of being one of the only two clients to be murdered after they had consulted Holmes, the other unfortunate being Hilton Cubitt of *The Dancing Men*.

One further comment on *The Five Orange Pips*. Let us whisper it very softly in case it should be heard on the far side of the Atlantic. The awful truth seems to be that Holmes did not know which one of the United States was the Lone Star State, and even Watson's Texas was qualified by the words 'I think.'

We now come to a period during which the two friends were parted. Between September 1888 and March 20, 1889, Holmes was summoned to Odessa in the case of the Trepoff murder, cleared up the singular tragedy of the Atkinson brothers at Trincomalee, and accomplished a delicate and successful mission for the reigning family of Holland. Watson only knew of these matters by reading the daily press. We are not specifically informed that Holmes actually went either to Trincomalee or to Holland, but presumably it was his departure to these places that was mentioned in the newspapers, for if he had contrived to solve either mystery without leaving London it is unlikely that any report would have appeared. As for Watson, his principal achievement during this period was to put on seven and a half pounds in weight.

On March 20, 1889, they met again, in connection with *A Scandal in Bohemia*. Our reasons for rejecting 1888 which is the year given by Watson to this case can be more conveniently considered in the next chapter. This was the famous occasion on which Holmes was defeated by that fascinating female, Irene Adler. As Watson says in his opening sentence: 'To Sherlock Holmes she is always *the* woman.'

It is generally considered that this case must in fact be earlier than *The Five Orange Pips* on the grounds that the latter refers to the glamorous Irene. John Openshaw had been told that Holmes had never been beaten. Holmes's comment on this was: 'I have been beaten four times—three times by men and once by a woman.' So far we believe no one has ever yet disputed that the woman referred to is Irene Adler.

But is there, in fact, any justification for this view? For a start, Holmes had a sincere respect and admiration for this attractive adventuress and was wont to eulogize her on the slightest provocation. To him she is always '*the* woman.' But here we have not '*the* woman' but '*a* woman.' We should have expected something warmer—more appreciative. It might have been, for instance, 'a woman, but what a woman!' or 'a woman, the peerless Irene Adler!' As it stands it suggests some much less exciting lady who defeated Holmes but failed to capture his imagination.

As a candidate for this role we would like to advance the claims of Effie Munro of *The Yellow Face*. This case, it will be recalled, was one of Holmes's few failures. It was a problem set by a woman which defeated Holmes. Need we look any further?

But even if the missing woman is not Effie Munro, there is still no evidence that she is Irene Adler. She may be someone whose case was never recorded by Watson. After all, we do not know who the three men were who beat Holmes. Why should not the woman be equally anonymous? Somebody perhaps in one of the cases mentioned incidentally? Take, for instance, the list of incidental cases mentioned in *The Musgrave Ritual* to which we have already referred.[1] Holmes introduces them with the very significant remark: 'They are not all successes, Watson.' Two of them refer to women—the adventure of the old Russian woman, and the case of Ricoletti of the club foot and his abominable wife. We don't somehow fancy the old Russian woman, but we suggest that there are possibilities about Mrs. Ricoletti, particularly in view of Holmes's remark quoted above. It may well be that the lady in question was abominable rather than glamorous.

With so many alternatives we do not feel that the case for the fair Irene has been established, and accordingly we adhere to the view that *The Five Orange Pips* is, as it purports to be, earlier than *A Scandal in Bohemia*.

A few weeks later we find Holmes announcing that he had some ten or twelve matters in hand, but with the exception of one which had been referred to him from Marseilles, they had few interesting features. Lack of interest, however, cannot be charged against the unreported Dundas separation case, where, at the end of each meal, the husband had acquired the unfortunate habit of removing his false teeth and hurling them at his wife who, in these circumstances, not unreasonably applied for a separation. The reason why Holmes's services were required is not altogether apparent.

We come now to *A Case of Identity* and to Miss Mary Sutherland of the heavy fur boa and the broad-brimmed hat with the large curling red feather, tilted in a coquettish Duchess-of-Devonshire fashion over her ear. This case probably occurred at the end of April for

[1] See page 35.

it was still early enough in the year for the fire to be alight. It was shortly after *A Scandal in Bohemia*, for Holmes said he had not seen Watson 'for some weeks,' and he produced a snuff-box of old gold with a great amethyst in the centre of the lid which he had received from the King of Bohemia for his services in that case. It must have been a real treat to feast the eye simultaneously on this snuff-box and on the Duchess-of-Devonshire hat.

Hosmer Angel, the missing bridegroom, appears to have vanished on Friday, the 14th. Unfortunately in 1889 April 14th fell, not on a Friday, but on a Sunday. In any event Watson's timetable cannot be relied on this time. According to the account which he gives, the bridegroom vanished on Friday and the advertisement announcing that he was missing appeared the very next morning in Saturday's *Chronicle*. Experience suggests that neither the bride nor the advertising department would proceed at this speed. Hence his memory is clearly at fault, and all that we can reasonably conclude is that the case took place during the later part of April.

In June of that year came first, *The Boscombe Valley Mystery* and then, *The Man with the Twisted Lip*. Watson does not tell us the year of the former case, but it took place after his marriage and therefore between 1888 and 1890. The murder occurred on Monday, June 3rd, which establishes the year as 1889 to the exclusion of 1888 and 1890. *The Man with the Twisted Lip* took place later in the same month. Here we are told that it was in 1889, but Watson goes astray again when he informs the opium-fuddled Isa Whitney that the date is 'Friday, June 19.' In 1889 the choice lies between Wednesday, June 19th or Friday, June 21st.

From this case one, at first sight, comes to the embarrassing conclusion that Watson did not know his own Christian name, since we find his wife calling him 'James,' whereas elsewhere he is invariably referred to as 'John.' Wives are, however, allowed considerable latitude in the names they bestow upon their husbands.

The Engineer's Thumb was 'in the summer of '89, not long after my marriage.' Assuming a marriage at the end of 1887, it was in fact eighteen months after. Nevertheless we are not prepared to antedate the marriage to '88. The case against this is considered in the next chapter. Here, all we need say is that he was invariably vague in his estimates of time and that considerable elasticity must be allowed to such a phrase as 'not long after my marriage.' We must not demand the same degree of precision that we might expect from some other writers.

New problems confront us when we reach the next case, *The Dying Detective*. Our information is that it was 'in the second year of my married life' and that it was 'a foggy November day.' This appears deceptively straightforward until we examine it more closely.

For we are faced for the first time with a new matrimonial problem. Hitherto whenever he has mentioned his marriage we have known that the lady in the case was the former Miss Morstan. His second marriage did not take place until 1902 and all the cases considered in this and the last chapter were published long before that date. But *The Dying Detective* was not published until 1913. So it could possibly refer to the second marriage.

It seems curious that he does not differentiate between the two. If he has in fact merged them, and is treating the two as a single unit, then we are still in the period of the Morstan marriage. Probably the true explanation is that though not published until 1913 the sentence was actually written prior to 1902 at a time when he had in fact only been married once, and that it was never subsequently revised.

It is most unfortunate too that this case occurred during the month of 'foggy November,' for in all probability Watson was married at some time in the month of November 1887, foggy or otherwise, but we do not know on which day of that month. Hence we are in difficulties with the description 'the second year of my married life.' If the case is on a later day of the month than the wedding, then the second year will be 1888. Conversely, if it is earlier the second year will be 1889. For two reasons the latter alternative seems the more probable.

In the first place we have already suggested that at the time of *The Resident Patient* at the end of October 1887 he seems by all appearances to have made very little preparation for matrimony. There is no hint of an approaching wedding. The distressing signs which indicate a prospective bridegroom are conspicuously absent. One would imagine that both bride and groom would be in favour of a church wedding and that the bride at all events would invite a certain number of guests. Even if we assume a registry office ceremony, there remain the more important questions of finding a practice and of setting up and furnishing a home. It seems reasonable therefore to allocate most of the month of November to these activities and to conclude that the wedding took place near the end of the month.

The second point in favour of the later year is, as we have already seen, that during the interval between the last case in 1888 and the first in 1889 both Holmes and Watson carried out programmes which would take a

certain amount of time to complete. We know that
Holmes travelled to Odessa, and in all probability he
also went to Trincomalee and to Holland. Presumably
there were intervals between these journeys. It would
indeed be a coincidence if directly he returned from
one he started off on the next. Watson too had an
agenda which required time. He had to put on seven
and a half pounds in weight. Now if *The Dying Detective*
occurred in '88, it would be the last recorded case in
that year, and the period during which the journeys
and the increase in weight had to materialize would
only extend from November to March 20th, an allow-
ance which seems inadequate for either purpose. On
the other hand, if the case occurred in '89, *The Five
Orange Pips* is the last case in '88 and the time period
starts from September instead of November. We have
thus two precious additional months which would
probably make all the difference, enabling both men to
complete their respective programmes without undue
strain. For these reasons we think that the correct
year is 1889.

Next in time we come to *The Blue Carbuncle* on 'the
second morning after Christmas.' There is a happy
nostalgic atmosphere about this episode from its commencement where Henry Baker makes his unsteady
journey down the Tottenham Court Road, carrying
home his Christmas goose, to its conclusion where
Holmes, having discovered the thief of the Countess of
Morcar's blue carbuncle, instead of handing him over
to the police allows him to depart with the comment:
'I suppose I am committing a felony, but it is just
possible that I am saving a soul. . . . Besides it is a
season of forgiveness.'

The same spirit of Christmas amity seems to prevail

amongst all who have written subsequently about the case. However much they may disagree about other dates, Monsignor Ronald Knox, Mr. Roberts, Mr. Blakeney and Mr. Bell are all in agreement that this is the Christmas of 1889. We can only associate ourselves with them. At the same time so much agreement is rather dull, and we cherish a secret hope that the next writer on this subject will unearth some evidence to show that we are all wrong and that *The Blue Carbuncle* in fact occurred in some other year.

The method of dating this case is as follows. It refers to *The Man with the Twisted Lip* and must therefore be later than June 1889. On the other hand, it is itself referred to in *The Copper Beeches* and must therefore be earlier than the spring of 1890. Hence the Christmas in question must be 1889.

In 1890 Watson saw less of Holmes than in previous years, and he tells us that there were only three cases of which he retained any record.[1] One of these three apparently was never published.

Probably the first of the three in time would be *The Copper Beeches*, for it was on 'a cold morning of the early spring' and therefore presumably in the month of March. It can be argued that this adventure of Violet Hunter of the rich chestnut tresses relates to the period prior to Watson's marriage and this argument will be considered in the next chapter. If, however, it is subsequent to the marriage the date appears to be March 1890, for as we have already seen it is later than *The Blue Carbuncle* and March 1891 is excluded, as apparently Holmes was at that time in France 'engaged by the French Government upon a matter of some importance.'[2]

---

[1] *The Final Problem.*   [2] *ibid.*

The remaining case in 1890 is *The Red-Headed League*. Here, for once in a way, it is not the year but the month that is in doubt. Jabez Wilson, the pawnbroker, answered an advertisement in *The Morning Chronicle* of April 27, 1890. 'Just two months ago.' As a result he was employed by the League for a period of eight weeks. But the notice telling him that the League had been dissolved, which meant that his job had suddenly come to an end, was dated October 9, 1890. So something seems to have gone wrong with the arithmetic.

It seems clear that it is the earlier month that should be discarded, for Watson says that it happened in the autumn. Moreover, in 1890 April 27th was on a Sunday, so *The Morning Chronicle* would not appear on that day.

It was on a Saturday morning that Wilson arrived at the office of the League and read the notice of dissolution tacked on to the door and dated October 9th. In 1890 this date fell, not on a Saturday, but on a Thursday. Yet, after all, there is no reason why the notice should bear the same date as that on which it was read by Wilson. Presumably John Clay gave the date on which he actually wrote the notice and it was read by Wilson two days later, i.e. on October 11th. The real mystery is why Clay ever made the fatal mistake of writing the notice at all. Whether Wilson was in fact employed for eight or for nine weeks and whether he received seven weeks' or eight weeks' salary is not entirely clear, but we can be certain that this arrangement started on either the 9th or the 16th August, and that April 27th is quite out of the question.

Here and there we observe signs of the changing

years. Greater intimacy has been established with Scotland Yard. Peter Athelney Jones of the Yard who was 'Athelney Jones' in *The Sign of Four*, has now become 'Peter Jones.' But increased intimacy does not bring increased respect, for he is still described as 'brave as a bulldog and as tenacious as a lobster,' but 'an absolute imbecile in his profession.'

Watson by now has forsaken his Paddington practice and has transferred to Kensington. The move took place at some time later than the summer of 1889 for he was still in Paddington at the time of *The Engineer's Thumb*. We have considered the possibility of a practice at Notting Hill Gate which might, at a pinch, qualify for both 'Paddington' and 'Kensington.' But this theory will not hold water, for the Paddington practice was near Paddington Station so that some of the railway staff were among his patients, whilst from his Kensington practice he walked *across* the Park to reach Baker Street. Notting Hill Gate scarcely meets either requirement.

We cannot leave *The Red-Headed League* without a word about the villain of the piece, John Clay, Old Etonian and grandson of a Royal Duke. On the whole, we think he is the most interesting of all Holmes's opponents of the male sex. It is true that he made the fatal mistake of putting up the notice which led to his downfall, but he was an artist in his methods, particularly in his economy of material. That alleged Napoleon of crime, Professor Moriarty, found it necessary to use an enormous network of assistants which stretched across the map of Europe from the Bentinck Street corner of Welbeck Street to the Daubensee above the Gemmi Pass. By way of contrast, the equipment of the Old Etonian was limited to a red-headed confederate, an empty office and the first volume of the *Encyclopaedia Britannica*.

From the account which he gives it seems clear that *The Final Problem* is the only case for the year (or more accurately fraction of the year) 1891 with which Watson has any concern. During the early months of the year Holmes spent some time in France on a matter of supreme importance at the request of the French Government. But he found time to engage in some preliminary skirmishes with Moriarty, who complained that Holmes had thwarted him on the 4th and 23rd of January, the middle of February and the end of March.

The ultimate struggle between the two as described in *The Final Problem* started on April 24th and continued until May 3rd. During this period Moriarty made several unsuccessful attempts to murder Holmes, but as far as Watson was concerned, the last straw was reached when their rooms in Baker Street were set on fire. Well might he exclaim: 'Good heavens, Holmes! This is intolerable.'

By the time he heard of this outrage he was in the train accompanying Holmes to the Continent. Moriarty followed them to Switzerland. On May 3rd they were at the Reichenbach Falls when a faked message was received which caused Watson to leave his companion and go down to Meiringen. Exit Watson, enter Moriarty. Holmes and Moriarty met on the precipice above the falls. Locked in each others arms they struggled together to the edge of the cliff above the rushing torrent.

That was the end of Professor Moriarty. That, too, was the end of Sherlock Holmes—for a period of nearly three years.

CHAPTER TEN

Marriage and its Problems

ఆశ్రా

So far the two main problems connected with Watson's first marriage have been allowed to stand over on the grounds that any attempt to consider them would be almost unintelligible until we had completed the chronological survey contained in the last two chapters.

These two problems may be summarized as follows:
(1) At the time of certain of the cases was Watson a bachelor, a married man or a widower?
(2) What was the date of his marriage?

So far as the first problem is concerned there are a certain number of cases which appear to fall in either 1889 or 1890 at a time when he was undoubtedly married, and yet he appears to be quite oblivious of his wife. Five cases in all seem to come into or near this category, but two of the five will not require very much consideration. One of these is *The Greek Interpreter*. There are some indications that this case comes into the period now under consideration, but we have already given our reasons[1] for rejecting this view and placing it back in 1882. They need not be repeated here. Nor need we spend any time on *The Valley of Fear*. On investigation this case turns out to be very much later and it can be more conveniently dealt with in the next chapter when we come to the affairs of Professor Moriarty.

[1] See pages 58–61.

We are left with the three cases in which there is a real conflict of evidence. *The Cardboard Box, The Copper Beeches* and *The Hound of the Baskervilles.*

Let us start with *The Cardboard Box* where we find a reference by Holmes to 'the investigations *which you have chronicled* under the names of the "Study in Scarlet" and of the "Sign of Four."' The latter case was not published until February 1890, when he had been married more than two years.

On the other hand, he makes no mention whatsoever of his wife. He is clearly living in Baker Street. The reason why he was not that August enjoying either the glades of the New Forest or the shingle of Southsea was a depleted bank account. If he had left Baker Street and had set up in practice he would probably not put the question in terms of finance but would say: 'my practice is never very absorbing.' He refers to 'our rooms' and 'our blinds,' whilst Holmes talks about 'your newly framed picture of General Gordon' and 'the unframed portrait of Henry Ward Beecher which stands upon the top of your books.' We are not specifically informed that the Beecher portrait belonged to Watson, but he was apparently an admirer of Beecher, and it is very difficult to read the paragraph in question on the basis that the picture belonged to Holmes.[1]

---

[1] This passage dealing with the episode of the thought reading and the Gordon and Beecher portraits has obtained considerable notoriety. It appeared first of all in *The Cardboard Box*. Later when certain of the cases were republished as *The Memoirs of Sherlock Holmes, The Cardboard Box* was omitted and the passage was transferred in its entirety to *The Resident Patient*. Later still when all the shorter narratives were collected in a single volume under the title of *The Complete Sherlock Holmes Short Stories*, it was restored once more to its rightful place in *The Cardboard Box*.

Again, the expression: 'Ring for our boots' precludes at all events a short visit to Baker Street.

Here unfortunately we cannot use Widower Watson to reconcile the differences between Bachelor Watson and Benedict Watson. After his wife's death he returned again to Baker Street and this could be the solution but for the fact that he did not return until 1894, whereas *The Cardboard Box* was published in 1893.

The absence of a wife, the sole ownership of the portraits and the books and the joint ownership of the rooms and the blinds can only point to one conclusion. The case occurred before he was married. It must be later than *The Sign of Four*, and therefore the only possible date is August 1887. The expression 'which you have chronicled' is an error which crept in at a later stage. Holmes originally simply made a comparison between *The Cardboard Box* and the two earlier cases. Watson in his rough notes jotted down 'Study in Scarlet.' and 'Sign of Four.' Later when he came to write his narrative of *The Cardboard Box* he made the mistake of anticipating the event and of assuming incorrectly that he had already chronicled the two cases.

Our next case, *The Copper Beeches*, was first published in 1892, so here again there are only two alternatives. If it does not come into the period when Watson was married it must be earlier. The later period is again excluded.

This time we are fixed much more firmly in the year 1890, for reference is made to five earlier cases, *The Noble Bachelor*, *A Scandal in Bohemia*, *A Case of Identity*, *The Man with the Twisted Lip* and *The Blue Carbuncle*. All but the first of these cases are dated 1889. To explain these away is no easy task particularly in view of the fact that *The Blue Carbuncle* reference is at a different place and in a different context to the other four.

The case on the other side is correspondingly weaker. As always there is of course no mention of Mrs. Watson, but the impressive catalogue of possessions in *The Cardboard Box* is completely absent. Instead of 'our rooms at Baker Street' we find 'the old room in Baker Street,' a phrase which in itself almost confirms that he was no longer living there. The only phrase which could possibly be construed as a reference to joint ownership is 'our gas,' an expression which a visitor who was receiving the benefit of the gas might well use.

It seems clear therefore that this case happened in March 1890 at a time when Watson was once more staying in Baker Street during his wife's absence. Probably she was again visiting that aunt of hers whom we have already encountered in *The Five Orange Pips*. Possibly this lady may not have approved of Watson who would thus not be included in her invitations. On the first occasion he mentioned casually that his wife was staying with her aunt, on the second as a sensitive man he preferred not to speak about the matter at all. Thus there is no mention in the case of Mrs. Watson.

With the last case, *The Hound of the Baskervilles*, there is a wider field of choice as it was not published until 1901. Dr. Mortimer, when he called at Baker Street in the absence of Holmes, left behind him his presentation walking stick. (It is curious how frequently Holmes's clients in these particular circumstances took insufficient care of their property. The result was always highly satisfactory, for Holmes invariably made a reconstruction of the missing client from the missing article.) The walking stick bore the date 1884 and in view of Holmes's remark 'five years ago—the date is on the stick' we appear at first sight to be in the year 1889.

But at once we come to the same sort of difficulties as we have encountered previously. This time it is 'our sitting-room,' 'our breakfast-table' and 'our visitor.' This time it seems clear that but for the unexpected visit to Baskerville Hall he would have been in residence at Baker Street from the beginning of October until the end of November. We have worked that aunt of Mrs. Watson's very hard, but we can hardly expect her to entertain her niece for two entire months. When it is decided that it is advisable for Sir Henry to have a companion at Baskerville Hall, Holmes proposes Watson without any reference whatsoever to either his wife, his home or his practice. When he gets there he writes Holmes letter after letter, all of great length, but he never apparently writes to his wife. In fact she is not mentioned throughout the fifteen chapters of *The Hound of the Baskervilles*. This omission, which can be overlooked in a short narrative such as *The Copper Beeches*, cannot be overlooked in a work of this length. The inescapable conclusion is that she did not exist at the time in question.

Our year cannot accordingly be 1889, and 1888 is excluded for the same reasons. The period from October to November 1887 also fails since this clashes with *Silver Blaze*, with *The Noble Bachelor* and with Watson's marriage.

How about 1886? If so, Holmes's remark 'five years ago—the date is on the stick' is badly out, for the date on the stick was 1884. That either Holmes or Watson could have mistaken a two-year period for one of five years seems highly improbable. Moreover, the two-year interval is in any case very unlikely. The stick in itself affords evidence against such a short period, for 'though originally a very handsome one, (it) has been so knocked about that I can hardly imagine a town practitioner carrying it. The thick iron ferrule is worn down, so it is evident that he has done a great amount of walking with it.' But quite apart from the stick, the description of Mortimer suggests that he has been for some time in Devonshire and is by now throughly settled down to his country practice, and to his hobby of excavating neolithic remains. He is, for instance, able to say that there are very few people within driving distance whom he does not know. For all these reasons we think that the two-year period must be rejected.

The only remaining course is to try a later decade and to transfer everything from the eighties to the nineties. This would mean that Mortimer left Charing Cross Hospital, not in 1884, but in 1894 and five years later in 1899 he consulted Holmes about the Hound, this of course being at a time in which Watson was once more living in Baker Street. The only difficulty here is the necessity of altering not only the date on the stick but also some five dates, ranging from 1882 to 1884, which occur in Dr. Mortimer's record in the *Medical Directory*.

The explanation seems to be first that Watson's handwriting was very bad, and secondly that he rarely, if ever, corrected his proofs. It seems that his figure '9' looked exceedingly like an '8.' (Another example of this occurs in connection with the date of *A Scandal in Bohemia*.) On the first occasion on which the printer saw this figure he decided probably after considerable hesitation that it was an '8.' Having once come to this wrong decision he would naturally repeat the error with each subsequent figure, being under the impression that even if this was incorrect Watson would rectify it when he read the proof. But Watson never bothered to read the proof and so the '9's' have remained '8's' to this very day.

There are two further points to be made in favour of 1899 as against an earlier date. The article in *The Times* which was used for the purpose of warning Sir Henry Baskerville was on Free Trade. Even 1899 appears to be about three years or so too early for an article on this subject, but presumably somebody at Printing House Square was slightly in advance of his time. An article on Free Trade in 1886 or 1889 would surely be quite out of the question.

The second argument for 1899 is the attitude of Lestrade towards Holmes. In the end Scotland Yard came to regard him with respect and veneration, but the process took time. When Lestrade arrives in Devonshire Watson's comment is: 'I saw at once from the reverential way in which Lestrade gazed at my companion that he had learned a good deal since the days when they had first worked together. I could well remember the scorn which the theories of the reasoner used then to excite in the practical man.' Lestrade had certainly not acquired this reverential attitude at the time of *The Norwood Builder*, a case which occurred in 1894. Half a dozen extracts to the contrary could be produced, but one must suffice. ' "Yes, some of us are a little too much inclined to be cocksure, Mr. Holmes," said Lestrade. The man's insolence was maddening. . . .' The inference is that the reverential attitude developed, as far as Lestrade was concerned, at a later date than 1894.

To sum up, it must be admitted that *The Hound of*

the Baskervilles is as difficult a case as any to date. There are objections to any answer that can be given but, all things considered, the best solution appears to be October-November 1899.

We come now to the second problem, a topic upon which more ink has been spilt than upon any other subject connected with the life of Sherlock Holmes. What was the date of Watson's marriage to Miss Morstan?

At the heart of the problem lie the two cases of *The Five Orange Pips* and *The Sign of Four*. The former case purports to be in September 1887 and as we have already seen, Watson's wife is away on a visit to her aunt, the latter is apparently in 1888 and it is then that Watson meets Miss Morstan who is later to become his wife.

At first sight our requirement would appear to be an extra wife, a lady who conveniently died in 1887, leaving him free to marry again in 1888. But actually this lady would not be of much help to us, for, quite apart from the marriage, *The Sign of Four* is referred to in *The Five Orange Pips* and therefore must be earlier in time. It is therefore common ground to all controversialists that this adjustment between the two cases must be made, so that *The Sign of Four* becomes the earlier of the two.

There are, of course, three possible ways in which this can be done. We can either

(1) Alter the date of *The Sign of Four*, a method adopted by Mr. Roberts,[1] or

(2) Alter the date of *The Five Orange Pips*, a method adopted by Mr. Blakeney, or

(3) Alter the dates of both cases, a method adopted by Mr. Bell.

[1] *Doctor Watson.*

The result of the first and third of these methods is an
1887 marriage. The second one gives us a marriage in
1888.

We think that the third course is the correct one,
provided always that the cases for the years 1888 and
1889, the first two years subsequent to the marriage are
placed in the order given in the last chapter. In particular it is necessary to transfer *A Scandal in Bohemia*
from 1888 to 1889. (This presumably is another
example of Watson writing an '8' which looked like a
'9.') Mr. Bell fails to make this adjustment with the
result that his reconstruction of these years is open to
many of the same objections that can be made against
Mr. Blakeney's.

In the first of the three alternatives which we have
enumerated *The Five Orange Pips* remains at September
1887, the marriage takes place some time before this
and *The Sign of Four* is pushed back to a still earlier
date, probably to June 1886. But Watson was still a
bachelor in April 1887 at the time of *The Reigate
Squires*, so it is clear that the marriage must fall between
April and September in that year.

This at once results in a head on clash with the most
reliable of all the cases in this particular matter, *The
Noble Bachelor*, which was in the beginning of October
and 'a few weeks before my own marriage.' Whilst a
man may be vague and inaccurate in his dates he is
not likely to forget the period in the year in which he
was married. One would be reluctant therefore to
overrule *The Noble Bachelor* even if it stood alone. But it
is in fact supported by two other cases. Neither *The
Resident Patient* nor the concluding events in *Silver Blaze*
can have taken place before October 1887 and at that
time Watson was still unmarried. For these reasons the

April-September marriage and with it the first of our three alternatives must be rejected.

The second scheme leaves *The Sign of Four* in 1888, fixes the marriage at the end of that year with *The Five Orange Pips* taking place in September 1889. This too falls foul of *The Noble Bachelor*. Lord St. Simon, who was born in 1846, was forty-one years old at the time of his marriage which therefore must have occurred in October 1887, 'a few weeks before' Watson's own marriage.

A still more serious objection is that two years, 1888 and 1889 have become telescoped with chaotic results. The following eleven cases which we have discussed in the last chapter are involved:—

1888

June.	*The Stockbroker's Clerk.*
July.	*The Naval Treaty.*
Summer.	*The Crooked Man.*
September.	*The Five Orange Pips.*

1889

March.	*A Scandal in Bohemia.*
April-May.	*A Case of Identity.*
June 3rd.	*The Boscombe Valley Mystery.*
June 19th or 21st.	*The Man with the Twisted Lip.*
July-August.	*The Engineer's Thumb.*
November.	*The Dying Detective.*
Christmas.	*The Blue Carbuncle.*

If Watson's marriage did not take place until the end of 1888, then ten at least of these eleven cases must fall in 1889. We know that *The Final Problem* is the only recorded case in 1891, and only three were recorded in 1890.[1] Two of these three are *The Red-Headed League*

1 *The Final Problem.*

and *The Copper Beeches*. This leaves one vacancy in 1890 which could in theory be filled by one of the eleven. Probably *The Dying Detective* would be the best choice.

Some of the results of cramming ten or eleven cases into a single year can now be considered.

(1) It ignores *The Blue Carbuncle* sequence. When this episode occurred, Watson remarked to Holmes that of the last six cases which he had added to his notes, three (*A Scandal in Bohemia*, *A Case of Identity* and *The Man with the Twisted Lip*) had been entirely free of any legal crime. This means that *A Scandal in Bohemia*, the earliest of the three is not more than six cases earlier than *The Blue Carbuncle*. But if all our cases are to be packed into a single year it becomes nine or ten earlier.

(2) Which is the earliest case subsequent to the marriage? If we are restricted to a single year it must be the March case, *A Scandal in Bohemia*, followed by *A Case of Identity*, with the June case, *The Stockbroker's Clerk* third at the earliest. On the other hand, if we are allowed two years, *The Stockbroker's Clerk* can be the first. The whole atmosphere of *A Scandal in Bohemia* suggests that Watson has been married for some little time. Wedlock suits him; he is putting on weight, etc. On the other hand, *The Stockbroker's Clerk* makes a strong claim to be first for the following reasons :

(*a*) Here and nowhere else does Watson give a short account of his activities from the time of his marriage up to the time of the case.

(*b*) Holmes remarks, 'I trust that Mrs. Watson has entirely recovered from all the little excitements connected with our adventure of "The Sign of

Four".' He would hardly leave this enquiry until his third reunion with Watson.

(*c*) He also expresses the hope that 'the cares of medical practice have not entirely obliterated the interest which you used to take in our little deductive problems.' This remark would scarcely be made if Watson had in fact given him the proof by assisting him with two separate problems within the last three months.

(3) The congestion in this congested year would be particularly acute in June with three cases falling within the first three weeks of this month. *The Man with the Twisted Lip* (June 19th or 21st) would presumably be the last of the three. Before this we would have to sandwich in both *The Stockbroker's Clerk* and *The Boscombe Valley Mystery*. If we assume that the latter is the earlier of the two, we encounter again all the difficulties previously mentioned, to which may be added Holmes's ignorance in *The Stockbroker's Clerk* of the arrangement whereby Watson's neighbour looked after his practice during his absence, a fact which would be within Holmes's knowledge a few days earlier, at the time of *The Boscombe Valley Mystery*.

On the other hand if *The Stockbroker's Clerk* comes first, a new difficulty arises. The journey to Boscombe (not the well-known seaside resort, incidentally, but a village near Ross in Herefordshire) must have taken place on either Friday 7th or Saturday, June 8th. The journey to Birmingham in *The Stockbroker's Clerk* was also on a Saturday, and would therefore have to be on June 1st. On this basis it seems improbable that Mrs. Watson would suggest that her husband looked pale and needed a change, when only a week before he had spent a whole day enjoying the delights of Birmingham.

(4) Presumably there was only one accommodating neighbour available to look after the practice, or Watson would use the plural instead of the singular. This duty was performed by Jackson in *The Crooked Man* and by Anstruther in *The Boscombe Valley Mystery*. The change from one to the other could have occurred during the course of a single summer, but it is far more probable that Jackson handled the practice in 1888 and that Anstruther attended to it in 1889.

Probably additions could be made to the four examples which have already been given if it were necessary. But it is not necessary. From whatever standpoint we approach the problem, it is all too clear that the attempt to pack two years' cases into a single year must fail.

Accordingly it follows that our second alternative fails, and that it is not sufficient to alter the date of *The Sign of Four* and to leave that of *The Five Orange Pips* unchanged. Both dates must be altered as also must be the date of *A Scandal in Bohemia*. When this has been done we get as our final result:

> July 1887. *The Sign of Four.*
> November 1887. Watson marries.
> September 1888. *The Five Orange Pips.*
> March 1889. *A Scandal in Bohemia.*

This arrangement will not satisfy those who maintain that the unknown lady of *The Five Orange Pips* is Irene Adler, but it has already been submitted that there is no evidence to support this proposition.

No previous reconstruction of Watson's first marriage has escaped from criticism, and this one will no doubt share the fate of its predecessors. With this somewhat chastening reflection we will bid the problem farewell and will proceed from matrimony to Moriarty.

CHAPTER ELEVEN

Mainly Moriarty

HOLMES disappeared in April 1891 and was not seen again until 1894. What had happened in the interval? First he had to dispose of Professor Moriarty. The two met in combat on the top of the Reichenbach precipice. But Holmes knew baritsu or the Japanese system of wrestling, with the result that it was the professor who went over the edge and into the torrent far below. This was followed by a spectacular climb up the cliff by Holmes, somewhat impeded by a series of rocks thrown at him from above by Moriarty's confederate, Colonel Sebastian Moran. Eluding the Colonel, he travelled for ten miles over the mountains in the dark, and a week later found himself in Florence with the certain knowledge that no one in the world knew what had become of him. Up to this stage there is no reason to doubt his story.

His subsequent adventures were narrated to Watson[1] when once again they found themselves together in Baker Street. His story was, that in order to avoid the last surviving members of the Moriarty gang, he travelled for two years in Tibet under the name of Sigerson. Whilst there he visited Lhassa and spent some days with the head Llama. Next he passed through Persia, looked in at Mecca and paid a short but interesting visit to the Khalifa at Khartoum, the

[1] *The Empty House.*

results of which he subsequently communicated to the Foreign Office. Then, returning to France, he spent some time in research into coal-tar derivatives at Montpellier, and he was apparently there when the news of Ronald Adair's murder brought him to London.

The rest of the story is told in *The Empty House*. The invaluable Mycroft with remarkable foresight had apparently paid the rent of the rooms in Baker Street during the whole intervening period of three years, with the result that Baker Street was available and ready for future operations. A trap was set for Colonel Moran into which he promptly fell. It would appear that he was the last of the Moriarty gang and that his arrest closed the entire Moriarty episode.

Can this version be accepted?

Before attempting to answer this question we must set out four separate mysteries which require solution.

First, whether or not the arrest of Moran meant the end of Moriarty's gang, it certainly did not mean the end of Moran himself, for he was still alive in September 1902.[1] How was it that the murderer of the Honourable Ronald Adair and the attempted murderer of Sherlock Holmes managed to cheat the gallows?

Secondly, how comes it that both the Moriarty brothers are called 'James?' Watson tells us that he had not intended to write *The Final Problem*, but that he had been forced to do so by some recent letters in the Press in which Colonel James Moriarty defended the memory of his dead brother, the Professor. But in *The Empty House* Holmes refers to the Professor himself as 'James Moriarty.' It is surely unusual to find two brothers bearing the same Christian name.

[1] *The Illustrious Client.*

The third problem is one which we have already considered in another connection[1] and which at first sight appears to have nothing whatsoever to do with Moriarty. It is the problem of the three 'second stains.' Why were there apparently three separate cases all known as 'The Second Stain?' We have already suggested that the only possible explanation is that there was only one actual case, and that the two brief references to a case of that name are in fact messages in code. But what were the messages?

Lastly how can one reconcile the Moriarty of *The Final Problem* with his namesake of *The Valley of Fear*? In the latter case which purports to be 'at the end of the 'eighties' Watson knows all about Moriarty, 'the famous scientific criminal,' but in *The Final Problem* (April 1891) he has apparently never heard of him. If *The Valley of Fear* is in fact 'at the end of the 'eighties,' then Watson must have a very poor memory, for by 1891 he has forgotten the very name of the super criminal. On the other hand if *The Final Problem* is the earlier of the two, it would appear that Moriarty as well as Holmes survived the Reichenbach encounter. In either event there is a mystery to be solved, and to eliminate one or other of the alternative mysteries, we must ascertain the date of *The Valley of Fear*.

Birdy Edwards came to Vermessa on February 4, 1875, and some three months later the Scowrers were arrested. Their trial would probably take place late in the same year. Ted Baldwin and his confederates were released after serving ten years of their sentences, so we may reckon that they regained their freedom in the autumn of 1885. Once outside they immediately turned their attentions to Mr. Edwards on whose life

[1] See pages 70–73.

two attempts were made whilst he was still living in Chicago. Not unreasonably he decided that California was a healthier climate than Chicago. The date of his departure to California is not known, but allowing a short interval for the two unsuccessful attempts in Chicago, it would probably be early in 1886. He must have been at least six years in California, for he was in partnership there with Cecil Barker for five years, and the first Mrs. Edwards died there in the year before he met Barker. The earliest possible time therefore for his departure from California for England is some time in 1892, and not during the first two or three months of that year. Seven more years rolled by in Sussex and then came the events described in *The Valley of Fear.* This brings us to 1899, but as we are told that the murder occurred on January 6th we can say with confidence that January 1900 is the earliest possible date for *The Valley of Fear.*

Further evidence that 1900 is approximately the right period is forthcoming in that Billy, the page, is functioning at Baker Street. We meet him again in the summer of 1903 in *The Mazarin Stone* and as at that time he was only a 'young but very wise and tactful page,' he cannot have started his career much before 1900.

The Valley of Fear could of course be later than 1900. If, for instance, Edwards had stayed for more than a year in Chicago before he decided to fly, or again he may have spent more than a year in California before his wife's death. But one is reluctant to travel further down the years in view of Watson's statement that it was at 'the end of the eighties.' Already we have a discrepancy of at least ten years. Surely that is quite enough. Moriarty, who should have been dead in 1891, is still apparently very much alive in 1900.

Having listed these four problems, we can now return once more to Holmes and can consider whether or not his story of his wanderings between 1891 and 1893 can be accepted. Did he in fact go first to Tibet, then to Mecca, then to Khartoum and finally to the coal-tar derivatives of Montpellier?

It would surely be asking too much of Holmes of all people at a moment's notice to cease his endless warfare against the criminal world and to bury himself in Tibet, Mecca, etc. for three years. Apparently he had never previously expressed any interest in these places or shown any desire to visit them, nor did he ever again refer to them. The more one considers it, the less real does this 'Tibet' episode become. In fact, to make no bones about it, we do not believe that he went either to Tibet or to Mecca or to Khartoum. Even Montpellier of the coal-tar derivatives seems distinctly doubtful though it has at least the merit of being in the right continent.

Where then did he get to during these three years, and why did he tell this extraordinary story to Watson? This is yet another mystery to add to our already lengthy list.

A solution to some of them can be reached on the hypothesis that the duel between Holmes and the Moriarty gang was a much more prolonged affair than would appear from Watson's narrative. It is not merely limited to the struggle culminating with the death of Moriarty in *The Final Problem*, the downfall of Moran in *The Empty House* and the events described at the commencement of *The Valley of Fear*. It was in progress during the three years interval between *The Final*

Problem and *The Empty House*, and it continued for many years after the latter, in a form which might be described by a more modern generation as a 'cold war.'

Holmes may have been guilty of an understatement when he told Watson that 'the trial of the Moriarty gang left two of its most dangerous members, my own most vindictive enemies, at liberty.'[1] Whilst clearly many members of the gang must have gone down with Moriarty, it is probable that many more survived and that the gang was able to continue as a going concern. Moreover a new leader had arisen to replace Professor Moriarty, a new Napoleon in the world of crime, who was to prove even more elusive than his predecessor. The first Napoleon made a single slip, a very small one, but it was sufficient to bring about his ultimate downfall. The second made no such mistake, and Holmes failed to bring him to book. His name? Colonel James Moriarty.

It is not now possible to reconstruct in detail the struggle between Holmes and the Colonel. Only a somewhat shadowy outline can be traced, and the gaps are all too many.

Probably Holmes realized right from the moment that the Professor toppled into the Reichenbach Falls that the gang would continue to operate under his brother, the Colonel. Far from burying himself in Tibet, the obvious course was to disguise himself, to mix with the gang and to fight them from the inside. We know that Holmes could never resist a disguise. At different times we find him masquerading as a plumber with a rising business,[2] a loafer,[3] an old salt,[4] a drunken

---

[1] *The Empty House.*   [2] *Charles Augustus Milverton.*
[3] *The Beryl Coronet.*   [4] *The Sign of Four.*

groom,[1] an amiable and simple-minded Nonconformist Clergyman,[1] an opium addict,[2] a venerable Italian priest,[3] a crippled bookseller,[4] an unshaven French *ouvrier* in a blue blouse,[5] a workman looking for a job[6] and an old woman.[6] Clearly therefore this would be the course he would adopt.

Probably it was fairly successful, for three years later he was able to emerge from his hiding place and return to London. No doubt many minor members of the gang received their deserts, but in the very centre of the web the spider still remained unharmed.

During these three years Holmes may have been dead to the world at large, but it is very doubtful if Scotland Yard took this view. Probably they knew of his underground warfare against the Colonel and were no doubt called in from time to time to arrest members of the gang. Consider, for instance, Lestrade's greeting to Holmes when they met for the first time after Holmes's return to London. 'It's good to see you back in London, sir.' This hardly sounds an adequate welcome for one returned from the dead. Lestrade seems to show no curiosity to know how Holmes survived the Reichenbach, and the assumption must be that he knew all about it already.

Did Holmes have any unofficial allies in his contest with the Colonel during these three years? Watson, we think, can be dismissed. The worthy doctor obviously believed that his friend was dead and as Holmes pointed out it was all important that he should think he was dead, 'for you would not have written so convincing an account of my unhappy end had you

[1] *A Scandal in Bohemia.*   [2] *The Man with the Twisted Lip.*
[3] *The Final Problem.*   [4] *The Empty House.*
[5] *Lady Francis Carfax.*   [6] *The Mazarin Stone.*

not yourself thought that it was true.' Moreover, to make an accomplice of Watson was clearly a risky proceeding. He had been so closely connected with Holmes that the Colonel would be certain to keep a close watch on his movements.

Mycroft Holmes, on the other hand, possessed obvious possibilities. Whilst everyone associated Watson with Holmes, few would look for a similar link between Mycroft and his brother. Mycroft appeared to dwell to such a large extent in his own little self-contained world, the boundaries of which were his lodgings in Pall Mall, his office in Whitehall and the Diogenes Club. Nobody would suspect Mycroft.

We already know that he was aware that Holmes was still alive, that he supplied him with money and that he had preserved the rooms in Baker Street and all Holmes's papers. It is therefore not unreasonable to assume that he played an active part in the war against Colonel Moriarty.

The details of this war will probably never be known, but it may have involved the sending of messages in code by Mycroft to Sherlock. We have already maintained[1] that there could not possibly have been three separate cases all involving a 'second stain' which was different in some way from the first, and that the only possible explanation of the references to cases of that name contained in *The Yellow Face* and *The Naval Treaty* is that they are part of a code. Both these narratives were first published in the year 1893 when Holmes, ostensibly dead, was actually waging his underground war against the Colonel.

This at once raises the question of the part played by Watson, since it was he who actually wrote *The Yellow*

[1] See pages 70–73.

Face and *The Naval Treaty*. That does not necessarily mean however that he knew anything about the code. He may have inserted the two passages at Mycroft's request without understanding their significance.

Probably in the early days of the conflict, before the Professor had been replaced by the Colonel, Holmes had anticipated that he would have to go into hiding, that Mycroft would assist him against the Moriartys, and that the only safe method of communication between them, in view of the many ramifications of the gang, was by means of a code. We do not know how Sherlock communicated with Mycroft, or for that matter, whether he ever found it necessary to do so at all. But messages in the reverse direction went through Watson, who was wont to embellish his narratives of Holmes's cases with brief references to other cases in which his friend had played a part. These references would form an admirable vehicle for conveying the coded messages.

Having invented the code, Holmes's next step was to ensure that Watson would co-operate in its transmission. Accordingly he told Watson of the existence of a code, without supplying him with any details. He was not even told that the code would deal with the activities of Moriarty. In fact probably at the time when the conversation took place, Watson had never heard of Moriarty. Holmes, however, stressed the point that at some future date he might have to go into hiding, that it might be essential for Mycroft to send a message to him, and as Mycroft would not know where he was, his only means of communication would be through Watson's publications. Such being the case, would Watson, please, co-operate by agreeing to insert in any narrative that he was about to publish, a paragraph which would be supplied by Mycroft, ostensibly referring to previous cases, but in reality being a message addressed to Holmes? Further, would he promise to do this in all circumstances, even if he believed that Holmes was dead, and even if Mycroft could supply him with no evidence to the contrary? Somewhat mystified and not in the least realizing what was involved, Watson gave his promise.

Among the symbols used by Holmes in his code was the 'Second Stain' which was of course suggested to him by the case of that name in which he had taken part in 1886. This probably represented some sort of an operation or enquiry which Mycroft was to carry out against the gang, the result of which had to be passed on to Sherlock. 'Operation Second Stain' was attempted by Mycroft for the first time late in the year 1892. It was a failure, and accordingly it was necessary to send some such message to Holmes as: 'Result abortive.' To his intense astonishment Watson was suddenly faced with a demand from Mycroft that he should publish immediately in his next narrative a statement that the case of 'the Second Stain' had been one of Holmes's failures.

The doctor of course protested. So far from being a failure, the 'Second Stain' had been a notable success. Moreover, what was the use of trying to send a message to Holmes when Holmes was no longer in the world to receive it?

Mycroft reminded him of his promise. Had he not promised Holmes that he would do so, even if he believed that Holmes was dead? Reluctantly Watson agreed. He was still quite convinced that Holmes *was* dead, and that it was a complete waste of time. But he could not break a promise which he had given to his dead friend. He may have tried to find out from Mycroft what the message was about, but if so, it is probable that Mycroft gave him a false, or at all events, an evasive answer.

The easiest way to perform his task was to write the account of one of the cases which actually had been a failure, so in February 1893 he published *The Yellow Face*, in which he made the false statement that *The Second Stain* was a case in which Holmes had erred. But for the activities of Colonel Moriarty, it is possible that *The Yellow Face* would never have been published at all.

A few months later Mycroft was again able to put 'Operation Second Stain' into action, this time with more fortunate results. On this occasion he found it necessary to write out the message himself. As delivered to Watson it contained a blank in which Watson was requested to insert the name of the case which he was actually writing. The message was as follows:

'I find them recorded in my notes under the headings of "The Adventure of the Second Stain" . . . and "The Adventure of the Tired Captain." The first of these, however, deals with interests of such importance, and implicates so many of the first families in the kingdom, that for many years it will be impossible to make it public. No case, however, in which Holmes was ever engaged has illustrated the value of his analytical methods so clearly or has impressed those who were associated with him so deeply. I still retain an almost verbatim report of the interview in which he demonstrated the true facts of the case to Monsieur Dubuque, of the Paris police, and to Fritz von Waldbaum, the well-known specialist of Danzig, both of whom had wasted their energies upon what proved to be side-issues. The new century will have come however before the story can be safely told. Meanwhile, I pass on to the second upon my list . . .'

In this passage, in addition to 'Second Stain' such words as 'Tired Captain,' 'first families,' 'Monsieur Dubuque,' 'Paris,' 'Fritz,' 'von Waldbaum,' 'specialist,' 'Danzig,' etc., may (all of them, or any of them) be code words which would convey a meaning to Holmes, and would tell him where the Moriarty octopus was vulnerable.

Watson, needless to say, regarded the proposal as fantastic. On the previous occasion he had been asked to make an untrue statement, now he was being asked to publish something which, so far as he was concerned, was complete gibberish. But once again he was loyal to the memory of his friend and to the promise which he had given. He was still convinced that Holmes was dead. Mycroft was undoubtedly mad, but in the circumstances the only course was to humour the lunatic. Inserting the words 'The Adventure of the Naval Treaty,' he incorporated the passage into the case of that name which was published for the first time in October 1893.

Had they known it, this message was the writing on the wall for the Moriarty gang. Though the leader bore a charmed life, the gang soon collapsed as an organization, and early in the following year Holmes decided that the period of the underground war could come to an end, and that the time was now ripe for him to resume life once more in Baker Street.

There followed the episode of *The Empty House* and the downfall, not of *the* Colonel, but of a lesser Colonel, Sebastian Moran. When the crippled bibliophile threw off his disguise and revealed himself as Sherlock Holmes,

Watson was so astonished that for the first and last time in his life he fainted.

Whilst the Colonel remained at liberty, Holmes was not able to disclose how he had passed the last three years. The Colonel must not know that it was Holmes who had reduced the gang to a mere shadow of its former self. Or if he did know it, the less he knew of the details, the better. Possibly too, Holmes had contact with some of the members of the gang, such as Porlock, the man who subsequently betrayed Moriarty in *The Valley of Fear*. Clearly therefore the true story had to remain a secret.

But some story had to be told to account for his absence, so he invented the journey to Tibet, etc. At the start the real facts were hidden even from Watson. This was a wise precaution. Watson, in view of his special position as Holmes's biographer, would be questioned by all and sundry who were curious to learn what had happened. There was a possibility too that he would have to give evidence at the trial of Moran since he was present at his arrest. In either capacity he might inadvertently let something slip which would put Moriarty on his guard. Clearly the best course was to keep him in ignorance until a certain amount of time had elapsed and the excitement occasioned by Holmes's reappearance had died down. So Watson was not let into the secret until some considerable time after Holmes's return. By that time, of course, he was fairly committed to the account that he gives in *The Empty House*, though this was not actually published until many years later.

What was the result of the trial of Moran for the murder of Ronald Adair, bearing in mind that we already know that he was still alive in September

1902?[1] An acquittal seems unlikely, for Watson says that the case for the prosecution was 'overwhelmingly strong,' and he writes of *The Empty House* as if it were one of Holmes's many successes which he would hardly do if Holmes, after procuring Moran's arrest, had found that he had insufficient evidence to obtain a conviction. It would seem then that he was found guilty and sentenced to death, but was subsequently reprieved. This act of clemency was not occasioned by any fondness of the Home Secretary for Moran, but in the belief that if his life were spared he would talk. He was to be the bait to bring in the larger fish, Colonel Moriarty. Unhappily for these optimistic hopes, Moran either could not, or would not, talk.

It will be convenient at this stage to move on ahead of the years, so as to dispose of the Moriarty story. Watson, still in ignorance of the facts, proceeded at once to write the story of *The Empty House*, Holmes refused to allow him to publish it. Possibly at this stage he may have been let into the secret. So *The Empty House* was thrown aside into a drawer to await a more favourable date, from where it was eventually resurrected many years later and published without any amendment.

Nor would Holmes allow any other case to be published. For the natural course was to start off with *The Empty House* as it would come first in time. If it were to be omitted and later cases were to be published the Colonel might perhaps smell a rat. The result was that nothing at all appeared in print after Holmes's return until a new century had dawned.

That it was Holmes, and not Watson, who exercised the restraining hand is evident from *The Norwood*

[1] *The Illustrious Client.*

Builder where we find Holmes announcing: 'Perhaps I shall get the credit at some distant day when I permit my zealous historian to lay out his foolscap once more—eh, Watson?' whilst Watson himself confirms this when he tells us that Holmes 'was always averse to anything in the shape of public applause, and he bound me in the most stringent terms to say no further word of himself, his methods or his successes—a prohibition which, as I have explained, has only now been removed.'

Meanwhile back in 1894, though not yet published, *The Empty House* had been already written, and a curious error had crept into the text which was not discovered until after the publication. In his conversations with Watson, Holmes had never referred to the Colonel as such. But once, in an unguarded moment he must have let slip the name of 'James Moriarty.' At once Watson jumped to the natural conclusion that 'James' was the Christian name of the Professor, with the result that there is a reference in *The Empty House* to 'Professor James Moriarty.'

Of course if he had only referred to his own account of *The Final Problem* he would have realized that 'James' was the name, not of the Professor, but of the Colonel. But then why should he? After all, at that time he only knew of the Colonel as one who had attempted to defend his brother's reputation in some articles in the Press. Apart from this he knew nothing whatever about him. Very soon he had faded into the background of Watson's memory and his Christian name was forgotten.

When Holmes enlightened Watson as to the true character of the Colonel, is a matter of conjecture, but it is clear that Watson knew the facts by 1900, the year of *The Valley of Fear*. By this time the gang had been reorganized, and it was operating as efficiently as in the days of the Professor.

Watson wrote his first account of *The Valley of Fear* soon after the case had ended. But the account which he wrote at that time was not the one subsequently published. There was no mention at all of Professor Moriarty. Instead it was Colonel Moriarty, who occupied the centre of the stage in the first two chapters and in the epilogue. Obviously Holmes could not agree to publication in that form. To quote his own words from *The Valley of Fear:*

'But so aloof is he from general suspicion—so immune from criticism—so admirable in his management and self effacement, that for the very words that you have uttered he could hale you to a court and emerge with your year's pension as a solatium for his wounded character.'

Watson was terribly disappointed. It was now 1901 and nothing had been published since Holmes's return in 1894. Holmes took pity on him and suggested that he should publish one of their more recent adventures, *The Hound of the Baskervilles*. This was an obvious choice, for Watson had already written Holmes a long report of his activities at Baskerville Hall, and if the rest of the case were to be dealt with at equal length he would be kept busy for a considerable time. The result was that *The Hound of the Baskervilles* appeared in serial form in *The Strand Magazine* from August 1901 until April 1902.

In the meantime the idea had occurred to him that by re-writing *The Valley of Fear* he could avoid the law of libel. Why not substitute the dead Professor for the live Colonel? He would add that the case took place 'at the end of the 'eighties,' and he would bring in Sebastian Moran and other relics of by-gone days.

The result is that the Moriarty of *The Valley of Fear* is a strange, composite creation, partly Professor and partly Colonel. It was, needless to say, the Professor who wrote *The Dynamics of an Asteroid* and who paid Moran a salary of six thousand a year. On the other hand it was the Colonel who owned the Greuze, whose rooms were visited by Holmes on three separate occasions, and who obliged the Scowrers by murdering Birdie Edwards.

But still Holmes was not satisfied. He was not prepared to risk even the revised version. It might still be held to be libellous if the Colonel could be identified under the mask of the Professor. Besides, libel apart, he did not want to warn the Colonel of a possible future line of action. Porlock was apparently the only traitor in the Colonel's camp at that time, but he might have a successor at a later date.

So once again publication was postponed, and once again in order to console Watson for his disappointment Holmes made a concession in another direction. He withdrew the ban on *The Empty House* which accordingly appeared in print for the first time in October 1903 in *The Strand Magazine*, to be followed by a dozen other cases in the ensuing months.

The Valley of Fear however, could not be published in the lifetime of the Colonel unless definite proof of his guilt could be obtained. Ultimately it too found its way into *The Strand Magazine* from September 1914 to May 1915, from which it would appear probable that the Colonel died early in 1914.

Holmes and Watson had resumed partnership at that time in order to defeat the German spy, Von Bork, and the doctor suggested that as the Colonel was now dead and the gang disbanded, no further objection remained to telling the story of *The Valley of Fear*. Holmes, however, pointed out that even now they had no definite proof of his guilt, so skilfully had he covered his tracks, and he felt that criticism might justifiably be made, unless they were in a position to substantiate everything that was said. To get over this difficulty Watson proposed publication of the narrative he had already written, which referred to Moriarty as the Professor. To this Holmes agreed. He was by now rather tired of the whole business, and was in fact much more interested in his contest with Von Bork. Hence *The Valley of Fear* as we know it to-day, with a Moriarty who is half Professor and half Colonel.

This brings the Moriarty saga to its conclusion. It may be that time will deal harshly with the theories advanced in this chapter. Maybe the future will reveal that the Colonel was a blameless and respectable old gentleman, that the 'Second Stain' was not a code, that Moran found some other method of cheating the gallows, and that two brothers had the same Christian name. But even if fresh evidence on all these questions is forthcoming, we shall still find it very difficult to believe that Holmes ever went anywhere near Tibet.

CHAPTER TWELVE

Back to Baker Street

WATSON was glad to be back in harness once more. That first evening when they went out to capture Moran was 'like old times when I found myself seated beside him in a hansom, my revolver in my pocket and the thrill of adventure in my heart.' Though he makes no mention of her death, it seems that his wife had died during Holmes's absence. As a result he was lonely and only too anxious to resume life with him in Baker Street.

He proceeded at once to sell his practice to a young doctor named Verner. The price was a high one but it was accepted without demur, for Verner bought the practice with money supplied by Holmes, a fact which did not come to Watson's knowledge until some years had elapsed.

The next three cases with which we are concerned can be dealt with simultaneously. One of them, *The Empty House* was a prominent feature of the last chapter. The other two are *Wisteria Lodge* and *The Norwood Builder*.

The Empty House was Holmes's first adventure after his return to Baker Street in 1894. According to Watson, Adair was murdered on March 30th of that year. His reunion with Holmes was on an 'April evening,' and in view of the exceedingly tall story that Holmes told on that occasion, the first day of that month would seem to be a very appropriate date.

The Norwood Builder took place when 'Holmes had been back for some months' and Holmes tells us how 'I crawled about the lawn with an August sun on my back.' Presumably this would be August 1894.

So far all is straightforward, but when we come to the third case, *Wisteria Lodge*, difficulties arise, for Watson asserts that it took place on a 'bleak and windy day towards the end of March in the year 1892.' Clearly this date is impossible. Holmes, according to his own account, was at that time in either Tibet, Khartoum or Montpellier. We have already expressed complete disbelief in his story. But it is even less probable that he was in Baker Street in 1892. Nor for that matter was Watson.

The first course, therefore, is to reject 1892 out of hand, and to look for some alternative method of ascertaining the date.

First, there should be no doubt about the month. For in addition to the statement that it was a 'bleak and windy day towards the end of March,' we are also told that it was 'a cold dark March evening.'

Next, we come to the reference to 'that little affair of the red headed men.' Hence it must be after October 1890. It cannot be March 1891, for at that time Holmes was in France, and in fact the only case in that year is *The Final Problem*. So it must be after the three years absence. In other words, it must be later than *The Empty House*.

On the other hand, it must be earlier than *The Norwood Builder*, for that case refers to the affair of 'ex-President Murillo' who is presumably the same person as 'Don Murillo, the Tiger of San Pedro,' the central figure in *Wisteria Lodge*.

So we can put our three cases in order of time, starting with *The Empty House* in April 1894 and ending with *The Norwood Builder* in August 1894. But in between the two we have *Wisteria Lodge* which unfortunately occurs in the month of March. The gap must therefore be widened, and either *The Empty House* must be at least a month earlier or *The Norwood Builder* must be at least a year later.

The former alternative is obviously the less drastic. Evidently *The Norwood Builder* comes soon after Holmes's return, for it is there that we are told how Watson sold his practice to Verner and rejoined Holmes. Again we are told that at that time 'Holmes had been back for some months.' If the months were, in fact sixteen in number, 'some' hardly seems to be the appropriate adjective. On the other hand, quite apart from its relationship to the other two cases there is some justification for assuming that *The Empty House* is earlier in the year than April. We are told that the murder of Adair was on March 30th, but outside his room was 'a bed of crocuses in full bloom.' The crocus is hardly likely to be blooming at the end of March, and it would seem that January 30th would be a more appropriate date. Watson's handwriting was not his strongest point and it is probable that his '4' was an L shaped creation which could easily be mistaken for a '2.' Hence '1894' easily became '1892.'

To sum up, we believe that the murder took place on January 30th of that year, and that our three cases can accordingly be located as follows:

February 1894. *The Empty House.*
March 1894. *Wisteria Lodge.*
August 1894. *The Norwood Builder.*

In between the last two cases we can insert *Shoscombe Old Place* which, for reasons to be given in the next chapter, we think must be assigned to May 1894.

It is in this period too that we find 'the shocking affair of the Dutch steamship, Friesland, which so nearly cost us both our lives.'[1] So shocking indeed was this episode that Watson could never bring himself to tell the world about it. It was something he wished to forget as quickly as possible.

Then again there was the enigmatic figure of Colonel Carruthers, one of the many who float before us for an all too brief moment, before vanishing into the unknown. In this particular case we are restricted to the single sentence, 'you know how bored I have been since we locked up Colonel Carruthers.'[2] Is this yet another criminal Colonel to be added to Sebastian Moran and James Moriarty? It is possible, but it seems unlikely that Her Majesty's Army would produce three such reprehensible characters of the same rank at the same time. It would be more charitable to assume that Watson is referring to our old friend Moran, and that 'Carruthers' was an alias used by that gentleman.

Later in that year 'on a wild, tempestuous night towards the close of November' the affair of *The Golden Pince-Nez* occurred. According to Watson this was one of many interesting cases which took place in 1894. There was the repulsive story of the red leech and the terrible death of Crosby the banker, the Addleton tragedy and the singular contents of the ancient British barrow, the Smith-Mortimer succession and the tracking down and arrest of Huret, the Boulevard assassin, an exploit which procured for Holmes a letter of thanks from the French President and the Order of

[1] *The Norwood Builder.*   [2] *Wisteria Lodge.*

the Legion of Honour. Unfortunately these cases were never published, and when Watson himself reminds us that he had three massive manuscript volumes for the year 1894, this is not surprising.

No information appears to be available for the first three months of 1895 but in April we come to 'the very abstruse and complicated problem concerning the peculiar persecution to which John Vincent Harden, the well-known tobacco millionaire, had been subjected,' and later in this month we meet Miss Violet Smith, a 'young and beautiful woman, tall, graceful and queenly,' the heroine of *The Solitary Cyclist*, a case which began on April 23rd and ended on the 30th.

At some time in this year a visit of several weeks' duration was paid to Oxford[1] during which the adventure of *The Three Students* occurred. No mention is made of the season, but May would seem to be the most appropriate month, when one considers the time-table of that memorable afternoon which immediately preceded the examination day for the Fortescue Scholarship.

Hilton Soames, according to his own account, was working in his study until four-thirty. He then went to tea with a friend and was away for rather more than an hour. On his return he found that someone had tampered with the examination paper. He questioned Bannister and decided to call in Holmes. The length of time that it would take him to come to this decision is open to conjecture, but he does not on the whole give one the impression of being a man who would make up his mind with undue haste. He then went to Holmes's lodgings, presumably a short journey.

[1] For evidence that Oxford and not Cambridge is the scene of *The Three Students*, see page 24.

More time elapsed during his conference with Holmes and Watson, after which all three returned to St. Luke's. 'It was already twilight when we reached the scene of our problem.' Holmes then carried out his investigation at the scene of the crime and he too interrogated the long-suffering Bannister. By the time they were out once more in the quadrangle 'three yellow squares of light shone above us in the gathering gloom' from the windows of the three students. There followed visits to Gilchrist and Daulat Ras, including in each case a sketch made by Holmes in their rooms and the breaking of a pencil during the process. The same performance would have taken place in the rooms of the third student, Miles McLaren, but for the fact that he told them (and, in our opinion, with some justification) to go to blazes and not to disturb him on the eve of the exam. By this time darkness had fallen, but Holmes's work was not yet done. He had still to visit four stationers' shops to see if he could procure a particular kind of pencil. By the time the day's work was finished he could say: 'my dear fellow, it is nearly nine, and the landlady babbled of green peas at seven-thirty.'

The programme outlined above is indeed a formidable one to compress within the limits of that portion of the day that extends from four-thirty to nearly nine. It is doubtful whether everything in the record can be taken at its face value. Soames, for instance, may have been mistaken in his times. But when all is said and done, and whatever revisions we may feel inclined to make, it is difficult to visualize this evening as occurring when the days are either at their longest or at their shortest. Moreover, it cannot happen during a vacation, and the last week in April is excluded, in any case, for that was the week of *The Solitary Cyclist*. May at once suggests itself as the most probable month. The only possible alternatives are the middle of March and the middle of October, and in both cases the days are probably too short.

Again May is better than either March or October from the standpoint of Gilchrist's long-jumping activities. He had already obtained a Blue for the hurdles and the long jump, whilst in his spare time he represented St. Luke's at Rugby and cricket. In addition to this he was described as hard-working and industrious. He was an entrant for the Fortescue Scholarship, an examination which lasted apparently several days and covered various subjects, and we should have had no hesitation in backing him to defeat both the brilliant but wayward McLaren and the methodical, inscrutable Indian Raulat Das. It will be seen therefore that his time was fully occupied.

On the afternoon in question he had been training for the long jump. It is unlikely that he would be occupied thus in October, as there would be no competition in prospect at that time. But in March he would be training for the Varsity Sports at the end of that month, and in May for the Amateur Athletic Championships and other important athletic events which take place in the summer. If the exam. were held in March, and as a result of the discovery that he had cheated, he were to be sent down, he would miss the Varsity Sports. Oxford would be deprived of the man on whom they relied to win, not only the long jump, but also the hurdles. This would be a disaster of the first magnitude, comparable only with the loss suffered by Cambridge a few years later when they were deprived of Godfrey Staunton's service on the eve of the Rugby match.[1] Oxford would be in an uproar. Bannister would have something to say about it. Soames would detach himself from Thucydides to lament Oxford's loss. Above all, Gilchrist himself would bewail his fate. But all three are silent. The inference must be that the worst disaster of all has been avoided, that the Varsity Sports are safely behind us and that we are in the month of May.

We cannot leave *The Three Students* without reference to an interesting theory propounded by Mr. Vernon Rendall in *The London Nights of Belsize*. He claims that *The Three Students* is not a genuine 'case' at all, but an elaborate conspiracy to hoodwink Holmes, in which Watson, Soames, Gilchrist, and Bannister were all involved. Holmes, it will be recalled, was occupying his time at Oxford on research in Early English Charters. Watson was afraid that overwork and worry would cause him to resume his drug-taking habits, so, as a distraction, with the aid of his three confederates, he staged a spoof job for him to investigate.

It is an ingenious theory, but the difficulties are formidable. Would the straightforward, matter-of-fact Watson be likely to concoct such an elaborate scheme? Would the highly respectable Soames be likely to take part in this hocus-pocus? What would his position be if Holmes were to go wrong in his efforts to solve the problem, and were to accuse one of the other two students of having tampered with the examination paper? Would Watson subsequently publish the case if it were not genuine? Above all, would Holmes, of all people, ever be deceived? Until further evidence is forthcoming we must continue to treat *The Three Students* as a bona-fide case.

[1] *The Missing Three-Quarter.*

Probably the whole of the month of May was passed in Oxford, for they spent 'some weeks in one of our great University towns.' The chief events of the next month were the investigation, at the express request of the Pope, into the sudden death of Cardinal Tosca, and the case of Wilson, the notorious canary trainer, whose arrest removed a plague spot from the East End of London.

'Close on the heels of these two famous cases' and 'during the first week of July' came the murder of *Black Peter* at Woodman's Lee near Forest Row in Sussex, a case which provides us with a picture of Holmes in his shirt sleeves with a huge barb-headed spear, stabbing at a dead pig swung from a hook in the ceiling to test whether or not it could be transfixed with a single blow. Athletic though he was, this achievement was beyond his powers.

The remaining case to be recorded in the year 1895 is *The Bruce-Partington Plans*. Holmes was at his best in its solution and Watson excelled in his magnificent description of the fog. The British public loves a fog beyond all things on earth, with the result that this particular one has tended to become a sort of standard background for Holmes's activities. In point of fact, fogs are not particularly common in Baker Street. There is one in *The Sign of Four*, but it is a rather anaemic affair. A better specimen occurs in *The Hound of the Baskervilles*, but its location is Dartmoor and not Baker Street. Holmes, of course, like most other people, functioned in all sorts of different weather. To take a few samples at random, we have the snow of *The Beryl Coronet*, the bright August sunshine of *The Norwood Builder*, the storm of *The Five Orange Pips*, the bitter frosty dawn of *The Abbey Grange*, the soft spring weather of *The Yellow Face*, the heatwave of *The Cardboard Box*, and the torrential rain of *The Golden Pince-Nez*. In another country any of these might have survived to become the standard Sherlock Holmes weather. But all have in fact been forgotten, and the survivor is the greasy, brown, swirling fog of *The Bruce-Partington Plans*. This is partly due to Watson's masterly description, but even more is it due to the fact that we, the English, love and cherish our fogs beyond all things on earth.

Apart from the fog, *The Bruce-Partington Plans* is also notable as being the case in which Mycroft Holmes makes his last appearance. Thereafter he apparently confined himself to his original isoceles triangle, bounded by Whitehall, Pall Mall, and the Diogenes Club, and Baker Street knew him no more.

The year 1896 is one which deserves a chapter to itself, but the earliest case in that year, *The Red Circle*, belongs to our present period and can be dealt with here. It is one of those cases in which Watson is silent as to the date. All that he tells us is that 'the gloom of a London winter evening had thickened into a grey curtain, a dead monotone of colour, broken only by the sharp yellow squares of the windows and the blurred haloes of the gas lamps.'

At first sight there seems to be no evidence available as to the year, beyond the fact that it happened at a time when Watson was living with Holmes. But valuable research has been carried out both by Mr. Blakeney and Mr. Bell, though they come to widely different conclusions. Let us consider their rival theories.

Mr. Blakeney thinks that it falls in the early period between 1881 and 1887. This theory is based solely

on the fact that the official side of the case was handled
by Inspector Gregson whom we first meet in *A Study
in Scarlet*, but so seldom see in the late years that an
early date must be assumed for most of his cases.

There is something to be said for this Gregson theory,
but not as much as Mr. Blakeney suggests. The difficulty is that it was Gregson who handled the affair of
Wisteria Lodge, which, as we have already seen, cannot
have taken place any earlier than 1894, and which in
Mr. Blakeney's own reconstruction did not occur
until 1896. How then is it possible to assume that any
case in which Gregson appears must be earlier than
1888?

On the other hand it is a fair assumption that he
retired soon after *Wisteria Lodge*. Both Gregson and
Lestrade were in *A Study in Scarlet* in 1881. Even at
that time it is probable that many years of service
lay behind both men. Lestrade, indeed, can talk of
little else. He tells us that 'I am no chicken' and that
'the old hound is the best, when all is said and done,'
and more specifically he speaks of 'my twenty years'
experience.' But it is Gregson, and not Lestrade, who
appears to be officially in charge of the case, for it is
he who writes to Holmes requesting his assistance.
Moreover, Holmes refers to 'Gregson, Lestrade, and Co.'
which suggests the seniority of Gregson. Again, when
Holmes mentions a case which had obviously occurred
long before the time of either man, it is to Gregson
that his question is specifically addressed. 'It reminds
me of the circumstances attendant on the death of
Van Jansen in Utrecht in the year '34. Do you remember the case, Gregson?' Of course he does not
really expect an affirmative answer. Clearly neither
man goes back to 1834, but the fact that, both being

present, the question is addressed to Gregson, suggests that he is the older of the two. At all events it is quite clear that there can be no very considerable disparity between the two, and that Gregson must have achieved something not far short of twenty years' service at the time of *A Study in Scarlet*.

Now we know from *The Three Garridebs* that Lestrade was still officiating in 1902, by which time he had completed forty years' service. It is unlikely that both men had such an exceptionally long career, and the probability is that Gregson had retired some years earlier. The year 1887 is, as we have already seen, much too early, but we think it reasonable to assume that he had departed from the scene before 1897.

We can now leave Mr. Blakeney and turn our attention to Mr. Bell. His selection is January 1897 and the main points of his argument are as follows:—

(1) It cannot be earlier than 1894. This is based on Holmes's remark to Watson: 'I suppose when you doctored you found yourself studying cases without thought of a fee?' This must relate to the period of Watson's marriage. It cannot possibly refer to the earlier period when Watson was an Army surgeon prior to his meeting with Holmes.

(2) It cannot be 1894. Mrs. Warren, the client, in her opening speech announces that 'You arranged an affair for a lodger of mine last year, Mr. Fairdale Hobbs.' This gentleman could not possibly have visited Holmes in 1893, and therefore Mrs. Warren could not possibly have visited him in 1894.

(3) It cannot be 1896, for during the greater part of that year Watson was away from Baker Street.

(4) Of the remaining years (1895 and 1897 to 1902 inclusive) *so far as Mr. Bell has been able to ascertain,*

1897 is the most adaptable from the standpoint of Wagnerian opera in London during the winter months. It will be recalled that at the end of the case Holmes exclaims: 'By the way, is it not eight o'clock, and a Wagner night at Covent Garden?' In January 1897 the Royal Carl Rosa Opera Company paid a visit to London, not to Covent Garden, but to the Garrick Theatre, and Mr. Bell concludes that this was the season in question, though he admits that he has only been able to obtain definite information for two years, 1895 and 1897. Watson, writing for publication many years after the event, quite naturally confused the theatres. Mr. Bell, accordingly, concludes that *The Red Circle* occurred in January 1897.

How far can Mr. Bell's conclusions as set out above be accepted? We can agree without reservation to the first two of his four points which exclude all years prior to 1895. We can also agree to the exclusion of 1895, as there does not appear to have been an opera season in London during the winter months of that year. Nor do we quarrel with his choice of a theatre. So far as we can ascertain there was no winter opera season at Covent Garden during any of the years under consideration, and as he says, Watson must have mistaken the theatre. So far we are in agreement with Mr. Bell, but we join issue with him on the last two points of his argument.

We do not think that the winter of 1896 can be excluded on the grounds that Watson was away from Baker Street at that time. All we know for certain is that he was away 'late in 1896.'[1] He was still living with Holmes in 'the third week of November in the year 1895,'[2] and whilst it seems probable that he was

---
[1] *The Veiled Lodger.*   [2] *The Bruce-Partington Plans.*

away for the greater part of 1896, there is no reason to believe that he had left as early in the year as January or February. The Carl Rosa Company had a winter season in that year at Daly's Theatre, including as usual a certain number of Wagner operas. *Lohengrin*, for instance, was performed on January 23rd and *Tannhäuser* on the 25th and 28th.

Even if Mr. Bell is correct in excluding 1896, he has still failed to establish the case for 1897. He says himself that he has only been able to obtain information for 1895 and 1897. Further research discloses a season at the Lyceum Theatre in 1899, including, for instance, a performance of *Tannhäuser* on January 3rd.

So far as the opera argument is concerned, therefore, there are at least three alternatives: 1896, 1897, and 1899. Probably if we were to investigate the matter still further, other possible opera seasons would come to light. But we do not intend to pursue this argument further. We think the time has come to pay our respects, so far as we are able to do so, to Mr. Blakeney's theory of Gregson's early retirement. In other words we require the earliest possible year, and that year is clearly 1896.

So with all regard to our predecessors, let us assert that the date of *The Red Circle* is January 1896, and let that hard-working servant of the public, Inspector Gregson, retire to a well-earned rest.

CHAPTER THIRTEEN

What Happened in '96

THE evidence of Watson's absence for at least some part of the year 1896 is contained in *The Veiled Lodger*, where we are told that 'One forenoon—it was late in 1896—I received a hurried note from Holmes asking for my attendance. When I arrived, I found him . . .'

So far as we are aware this is the only specific reference ever made by Watson to the year 1896. No other case is recorded for that year, and so far as his own dates supply our information, except for this case, there is a gap between *The Bruce-Partington Plans*, 'in the third week of November in the year 1895' and *The Abbey Grange* 'during the winter of '97.' Into this gap we have already inserted *The Red Circle* in January 1896, and we shall at a later stage include another case, *The Sussex Vampire*. Watson's silence suggests that he was away for the greater part of the year and that he departed very soon after the episode of *The Red Circle*.

Why did he go? Did matrimony claim him again? If so, he must have been married three times in all and his first two marriages would both have been of very brief duration. The first could scarcely have exceeded six years and this one would only be of a few months' duration. A succession of such short-lived marriages seems on the face of it improbable; after all we are dealing with John H. Watson, M.D.—not with

Bluebeard. Besides he never mentions the new lady, whereas the first Mrs. Watson is referred to on many occasions. Surely if he were forsaking her for a few days in order to assist Holmes in *The Veiled Lodger* we should get the same sort of explanation to account for his absence as used to be forthcoming when he parted company from the first Mrs. Watson to help Holmes in such cases as *The Stockbroker's Clerk*, *The Five Orange Pips*, or *The Boscombe Valley Mystery*. Nor when he is once more back with Holmes at the beginning of 1897 does he act or talk as a man who has suffered a recent bereavement. Reluctantly we fear that this romantic theory of a third Mrs. Watson must be jettisoned.

A more probable explanation of his silence is that there was something that he did not wish to divulge. This at once suggests a difference of opinion between Watson and Holmes leading to a temporary estrangement. Watson would probably regard it as bad form to make any reference to this quarrel in his narratives. Silence would be more dignified and more English.

What then was the cause of the quarrel? The fault was probably on both sides. Each man had his own particular weakness. Had they both shared the same vice, the trouble might never have arisen. But Holmes was a drug-addict whilst Watson was a gambler, and neither man was over tactful on the shortcomings of the other. Watson did not hesitate to express his views on the subject of cocaine and this may have been a factor in the case. But it was probably not the main cause of the trouble, for, after all, Holmes had been taking drugs, with Watson's knowledge, since the early days of their acquaintance, so that by this time he should have been getting accustomed to this eccentricity. On the other hand, Watson's interest in gambling was a much more recent phenomenon, and it was probably this which precipitated the crisis.

The evidence that Watson was a reckless gambler is contained in the two undated cases, *Shoscombe Old Place* and *The Dancing Men.* Elsewhere he appears as a cautious, steady character, and it comes as a severe shock to encounter in *Shoscombe Old Place* the following passage:—

'By the way, Watson, you know something of racing?'

'I ought to. I pay for it with about half my wound pension.'

We might be disposed to dismiss this as an exaggeration not intended to be taken seriously, but for the fact that *The Dancing Men* discloses that he had found it advisable to hand over his cheque book to Holmes who kept it locked up in his drawer. 'Your cheque-book is locked in my drawer, and you have not asked for the key.'

Our next task is to ascertain the dates of these two cases. *The Dancing Men* is the easier of the two. The month is July, for Hilton Cubitt says 'about a month ago, at the end of June, I saw for the first time signs of trouble.' As for the year there are only two possibilities, for he tells us that 'Last year I came up to London for the Jubilee.' It must therefore be either 1888 or 1898, and since Watson was living with Holmes at the time, the probabilities are heavily in favour of the later year, for in 1888 Watson had left Baker Street as the result of his first marriage.

So far as *Shoscombe Old Place* is concerned, we can start with the passage quoted above and with the fact that he has a wide and extensive knowledge of horse racing, sufficient in fact to qualify as Holmes's 'Handy Guide to the Turf.'

When did he first acquire this knowledge? Was he, for instance, equally learned on equine matters at the time of the other great racing case, *Silver Blaze*, a case which occurred in October 1887, only a month or so before his marriage? Let us travel back in time to 1887 and betake ourselves to Winchester accompanied by our 'Handy Guide to the Turf,' in order that we may find out if he was equally erudite on that occasion.

In the first place there is no record that he backed a single horse during the entire course of the afternoon. Holmes, on the other hand, had a bet on the race that followed the Wessex Cup. (There is no evidence that Holmes actually backed Silver Blaze to win the Wessex Cup, but knowing Holmes, and knowing what Holmes knew about Silver Blaze, we should be very surprised if he had neglected this opportunity.)

We have referred to the race won by Silver Blaze as the Wessex Cup. But *was* it? Watson refers to it on the same page, first as the 'Wessex Cup' and then as the 'Wessex Plate.' If he knew much about racing, one would expect him to know the correct name of a race which was evidently one of the major events of the racing season, for the disappearance of the favourite, a few days before the race, was 'the one topic of conversation through the length and breadth of England.'

The Wessex Cup (Plate) is described as a race for four- and five-year olds. With all due respect to the doctor this seems highly improbable. Two-year olds are segregated and there are many races which are only open to three-year olds. But beyond the age of three, there are no reservations in favour of particular years.

Next, as to the racing colours. We are given what purports to be a copy of the race card, but it in fact

appears to have been compiled after the event, and
from memory, by someone who was not accustomed
to studying racing colours. Of the six starters only two,
Silver Blaze and The Negro, appear to be sufficiently
and adequately equipped. Pugilist has a pink cap and
blue and black jacket. This might get past Messrs.
Weatherby and Sons who are responsible for the
registration of racing colours, but we think it very
doubtful. 'Blue and black jacket' is not sufficient. It
should be 'blue and black stripes,' or 'blue and black
hoops,' or 'blue and black quarters,' or possibly 'blue,
black sleeves.' Iris seems to be short of a cap, for his
description is merely 'yellow and black stripes.'
Desborough, 'yellow cap and sleeves' appears to be
even more exiguously clad, and Rasper, 'purple cap,
black sleeves' is in the same precarious situation.
Surely a racing man, accustomed to studying the
colours on his race card, would realize that something
else is required to connect the two sleeves?

Finally, there is the question of Desborough's odds.
We are told that the ring roared 'Fifteen to five against
Desborough!' There are a few examples of unreduced
fractions sanctioned by long usuage in racing odds,
such as '6 to 4,' '100 to 8,' and '100 to 6,' but *not* we
submit '15 to 5.' This we cannot accept in any
circumstances whatsoever.

To conclude, it seems clear beyond all possible doubt
that Watson was not a racing man at the time of
Silver Blaze or at the time of his first marriage. How
long an interval elapsed after that date, before he
started on the primrose path is unknown, but in any
event he was living in Baker Street with Holmes at the
time of *Shoscombe Old Place*, so that case cannot have
occurred before 1894.

On the other hand *Shoscombe Old Place* must be earlier than *The Dancing Men*, for if events had already come to such a pass that it was necessary for Holmes to lock up Watson's cheque book, he would hardly ask the question: 'By the way, Watson, you know something of racing?'

It would seem then that the sequence of events can be reconstructed as follows:—Watson first took to racing as a consolation for the loss of his wife and his separation from Holmes. By the time he rejoined Holmes in February 1894 he was deeply involved. *Shoscombe Old Place* happened very soon afterwards, at a time when Holmes knew that Watson had become interested in racing, but had not yet realized the full extent of the malady. Holmes of all people would be unlikely to remain in ignorance for any length of time, so we can be certain that this incident occurred very shortly after their return, probably in the year 1894. Thereafter Holmes allowed events to take their course for a time, but ultimately he remonstrated with Watson, warned him of the error of his ways, and probably even went as far as to suggest that he should take custody of Watson's cheque book. Watson resented this. What right had Holmes, the slave of drugs, to lecture Watson, the slave of the Turf? A row developed, and early in 1896 Watson shook the dust of Baker Street from off his feet. For some months they remained apart, but the experiment was not a success. They began to miss each other and to yearn for the companionship of the past. At the end of the year when Watson received a request from Holmes to rejoin him on the occasion of *The Veiled Lodger* he was only too glad to do so. When the case had ended he stayed on with Holmes, and realizing that he must endeavour to

subdue his gambling propensities, he was even prepared
to entrust his cheque book to him. Both men realized
that this somewhat drastic treatment was necessary.
The cheque book, accordingly, disappeared into
Holmes's drawer. We do not know how long it remained
there, but it was apparently still there in July 1898 at
the time of *The Dancing Men*.

If the above reconstruction is correct it follows that
the only possible years for *Shoscombe Old Place* are 1894,
1895, or 1896. We have already expressed a strong
preference for 1894, but we can go further and eliminate
the other two years.

It was 'a bright May evening' when they travelled
down to Shoscombe, so 1896 is only possible if Watson's
quarrel with Holmes and his departure from Baker
Street occurred later than April in that year. This
seems very improbable. Having once decided to cut
adrift from Holmes his pride would prevent him from
returning until a substantial interval had elapsed.
Yet we find that he did return 'late in 1896.' We can
therefore conclude that he left early in that year,
possibly in February, soon after the case of *The Red
Circle*. Moreover, his absence during the greater part
of the year is confirmed by the fact that *The Veiled
Lodger* is the only case mentioned in 1896.

The year 1895 can also be eliminated. This was the
year of *The Three Students*[1] when they spent 'some weeks'
in Oxford. Probably this visit extended over the whole
of the month of May. On the most conservative estimate, it would cover the first three weeks of the month.
But the visit to Shoscombe must also have taken place
during the first three weeks of the month of May, for
otherwise we should be very close to the Derby, and if

[1] See pages 131–134.

this were so, it would be impossible for two racing men, Watson and the trainer, John Mason, to meet without discussing the Derby situation, as such.

But, in fact, when they do meet there is no general discussion on the race, only a necessary and general statement by Mason that Shoscombe Prince is a prospective runner, and that Sir Robert Norberton has backed him with everything that he can beg or borrow. Clearly then the annual Derby fever has not yet reached its height, and we are still a week or two ahead of the race. There is thus a clash between Shoscombe and Oxford, and since Holmes and Watson cannot be in both places at the same time, we can rule out the year 1895.

This leaves 1894 as the only possibility for *Shoscombe Old Place*.

We can now return once more to 1896. What did Holmes do during Watson's absence? Obviously, very little information is available. No case in which Watson played an active part can fall within that period. But what of those which are only mentioned incidentally? One, and one only, shows some indication of belonging to the missing year 1896. We refer to the episode of Matilda Briggs which is mentioned in *The Sussex Vampire*. Evidently Watson had no knowledge of this case. He was apparently under the impression that Matilda Briggs was a young woman, whereas she was in fact a ship, associated, somewhat ominously, with the giant rat of Sumatra, 'a story for which the world is not yet prepared.' Perhaps his ignorance can be explained by absence.

This naturally brings us to *The Sussex Vampire* itself. We meet once again a familiar situation. Holmes and Watson are living together. No date is given. The month this time is November. The letter which introduces Ferguson is dated the 19th of that month.

One thing at least is certain. This is *not* an early case. Watson and Ferguson must have been approximately of the same age, for they were old opponents of the Rugby field. They had crossed swords in that memorable encounter between Blackheath and Richmond 'when I (Ferguson) threw you (Watson) over the ropes into the crowd at the Old Deer Park.' But since those far off days quite a lot has happened. Ferguson comes to the point with that same vigorous directness of approach that he displayed at the Old Deer Park—'Hullo, Watson. . . . you don't look quite the man you did when I threw you over the ropes, etc.' Watson is equally candid. It was painful 'to meet the wreck of a fine athlete whom one has known in his prime. His great frame had fallen in, his flaxen hair was scanty, and his shoulders were bowed.'

Of course there was another factor which might possibly account for the scanty hair and the bowed shoulders. The unfortunate Ferguson was under the impression (luckily erroneous) that his wife was a vampire. True, a belief that one's wife is a vampire is not on the whole likely to have a beneficial effect on either the shoulders or the scalp. Yet, when all is said and done, it does not seem fair to lay all the blame on the female Dracula. Some of the trouble must, we suggest, have been due to the passing years.

The most interesting feature of *The Sussex Vampire* is Holmes's reference on two separate occasions to his 'Agency,' the word being spelt each time with a capital 'A.' First we have: 'This Agency stands flat-footed upon the ground and there it must remain,' and this is followed by: 'We must not let him think that this Agency is a home for the weak-minded.' Search where we will there is no mention of the Agency elsewhere, and it must be something more than a coincidence that the only two references to it should both occur in the same case. Can the explanation have something to do with the missing year 1896?

On Watson's departure, Holmes would probably feel the need for a successor. This successor may have had advanced ideas. Not for him the cigars in the coalscuttle and the tobacco in the toe of a Persian slipper. Unanswered correspondence transfixed by a jackknife to the mantelpiece?[1] Preposterous! Something must be done about it. Business efficiency must be introduced forthwith. There must be a reorganization. Anyway, why 'Sherlock Holmes'? Why not 'The Sherlock Holmes Agency?' a far more impressive title.

Holmes was not impressed, but he was prepared to give it a trial. He always had a penchant for any new experiment. So for a time the new broom swept clean, and the Agency came into being. But the newcomer had underestimated the vitality of the jack-knife and the Persian slipper. Holmes soon tired of business efficiency and began to long for the return of Watson. Before long the new broom had departed and Watson was back once more, assisting Holmes to unravel the mystery of *The Veiled Lodger*.

Once he had returned there could be little doubt that the temporary visit would soon develop into permanent residence once more in Baker Street. This had occurred at the time of *The Sussex Vampire*, but so recently that Holmes was still talking about the Agency. We know that the first letter in *The Sussex Vampire* was dated November 19th. The year, though

[1] *The Musgrave Ritual.*

not mentioned, must accordingly be 1896. We also know that *The Veiled Lodger* occurred 'late in 1896.' It can safely be assumed that it was early in the month of November of that year.

So ended the great quarrel of 1896. The identity of Watson's substitute has never been disclosed. But whoever he may have been, he was attempting the impossible. There was only one man in the world adequately equipped to play the part of John H. Watson.

CHAPTER FOURTEEN

Back Again to Baker Street

DID Watson ever regret his return to Baker Street? Perhaps he may have done so two months later when 'on a bitterly cold and frosty morning during the winter of '97,' Holmes hauled him out of bed to take part in the matter of *The Abbey Grange*. This sounds very like January weather, and confirmation is forthcoming in the previous history of Lady Brackenstall, née Mary Fraser, for we are informed (*a*) that eighteen months had elapsed since she had arrived in England from Australia, and (*b*) that her ship, *The Rock of Gibraltar*, arrived in June 1895. This would appear to fix the date of *The Abbey Grange* as January 1897.

Anxiety for his old friend's health may have been one of the reasons which caused Watson to join forces with him once more. At all events in March of that year Dr. Moore Agar, of Harley Street, ordered him to take a complete rest, forthwith. Accompanied by the ever faithful Watson he took a small cottage at Poldhu Bay in Cornwall, and with his habitual unfailing versatility plunged into a study of the ancient Cornish language which he suggested was akin to the Chaldean, and had been largely derived from the Phoenician traders in tin.

But as the reader may have anticipated, the Cornish language had about as much chance of claiming his undivided attention, as had, on an earlier occasion, the Early English Charters. Fate had decreed that Holmes should never enjoy a holiday without interruption. Baker Street could never be left behind. It followed him wherever he went with a peculiar persistency. At Reigate it appeared in the shape of *The Reigate Squires*, at Oxford as *The Three Students* and at Poldhu Bay in the more sinister aspect of *The Devil's Foot*.

Holmes's illness which necessitated this holiday may well have been due to 'constant hard work of a most exacting kind.' But it would seem probable that his drug-taking habits were also a factor, and that this illness was what Watson had in mind when later in the same year, in the case of *The Missing Three-Quarter*, he expressed anxiety, lest idleness might lead to a further outbreak.

The Missing Three-Quarter was first published in 1904, and we are informed that it opened on 'a gloomy February morning some seven or eight years ago.' The month, however, must be wrong, for this case centres on the Oxford *v.* Cambridge Rugby match, which in those days, as at the present time, was played in December.

We are told that 'Oxford won by a goal and two tries.' The Cambridge score is not mentioned, but presumably it was non-existent.

The match must in any case have occurred after 1894, because Holmes talks of Armstrong as a man 'calculated to fill the gap left by the illustrious Moriarty,' (this of course refers to Professor Moriarty and *not* to Colonel Moriarty.[1] The Colonel had not yet attained the exalted position previously occupied by his brother in the world of crime. That was still two or three years ahead).

Our requirements therefore are a year probably

[1] See Chapter XI.

about seven or eight years before 1904, with 1894 as the limit, in which Oxford won the match, if possible by a goal and two tries to nil.

It must be admitted at once that the last requirement is beyond our resources. Up to 1904 Oxford had never beaten Cambridge by a goal and two tries to nil. On the other hand Cambridge had beaten Oxford by that exact score, on no less than five separate occasions, though only the last of the five, the match of 1898, comes within the period with which we are concerned. But clearly 1898 will not meet the bill. We do not see our way to accept a Cambridge victory in any circumstances whatsoever, not even one which gives the correct score—in reverse. Watson might easily be wrong about the score, particularly as he was not a spectator at the match. But when the surrounding circumstances of Godfrey Staunton's sensational disappearance are taken into consideration, he could not possibly be wrong about the result.

Failing the exact result, the next best thing is an Oxford win with a score as near as possible to the one given by Watson. After eliminating (*a*) Cambridge wins, (*b*) drawn games, and (*c*) those years which are too close to 1904 to come within the category of 'some seven or eight years ago,' we are left with only two years, 1896, when Oxford won by two goals to a goal and a try, and 1897, when they won by two tries to nil. Obviously the later year is closer to Watson's version. He is correct in all respects, except that he has overlooked Oxford's goal. In the circumstances it seems clear that *The Missing Three-Quarter* must have taken place in December 1897.

Two interesting cases occurred in the summer of 1898, *The Retired Colourman* and *The Dancing Men*. The reasons for placing the latter case in this year have already been submitted.[1] All that need be said here is that Hilton Cubitt's first visit to London was at the end of July, and that the journey to Ridling Thorpe Manor was some sixteen days later, and therefore in the middle of August.

The month of *The Retired Colourman* is not known. The only information is that 'on a summer afternoon I set forth to Lewisham.' It may be before or after *The Dancing Men*, but since this case occurred late in the summer the probability is that *The Retired Colourman* is the earlier of the two.

The year of *The Retired Colourman* presents no difficulty. Josiah Amberley married an attractive wife 'early in 1897.' The future looked rosy, but things went wrong, and so 'within two years' he was a broken miserable creature. Hence the year is 1898.

Holmes was unable to accompany Watson to Lewisham because he was fully occupied with an intriguing affair, involving two Coptic Patriarchs.

The situation in 1899 bears some resemblance to the preceding year, for again there are two reported cases, one of which we have considered at an earlier stage.

The Hound of the Baskervilles would appear from Watson's account to have occurred in the months of October and November 1889. But it has already been submitted that this year should be amended to 1899.[2] All that need be noted here are the extremely lengthy and comprehensive reports which Watson, writing from Baskerville Hall, sent to Holmes, to which may be added the long and equally detailed diary which he kept at the time. Taken together, they form an admirably complete and comprehensive record. Watson

[1] See page 143.   [2] See pages 99–103.

noted down everything possible about the places visited, the people he encountered and the events in which he and they took part. No detail was too trivial to omit, whether or not it might appear to have any bearing on the central problem of who (or what) was responsible for Sir Charles Baskerville's death. One has only to read the reports and the diary, which was presumably intended to form the basis of a further report, to realize that very few men in his position would have adopted a similar course. But Watson was clearly taking no chances. He was not going to be reproached by Holmes for a failure to supply *all* the relevant evidence.

Why was he so careful on this occasion? Was this his habitual procedure when Holmes was not on the scene of action, and he (Watson) was acting as his deputy? The answer, let us hope, to both of these questions, but certainly to the second of the two, is to be found in the case of *Lady Frances Carfax*.

This again is one of the undated cases, but the field is narrowed to a certain extent, for the Rev. Dr. Shlessinger (better known in some circles as 'Holy Peters') had been badly bitten in the left ear in a fight in a saloon at Adelaide in 1889, and as the usual evidence is available that Watson was living in Baker Street at the time of the case, we can say that the earliest possible year is 1894.

Now this ecclesiastical ear had been a source of trouble to poor Watson. Sent out to Lausanne by Holmes to investigate the case, he had sent in a report which mentioned Dr. Shlessinger. The result was a telegram from Holmes asking for a description of his left ear. Watson, inadequately instructed in the details of saloon-fights in the city of Adelaide, failed to see the relevance of this request, which was ascribed to mis-directed humour on the part of Holmes. No action was taken and the result was, to say the least of it, un-fortunate. Holmes's comments on the subject were terse and to the point.

For a short time following this misadventure Watson would bear it in mind, and he would take every precaution to avoid repeating the same mistake. But after a year or so had passed, it would recede from his memory and he would revert to normal. This indicates that *Lady Frances Carfax* happened in 1899, very shortly before *The Hound of the Baskervilles*. We can assume that it was in the summer months, for our clerical friend with the injured ear spent his days 'upon a lounge-chair on the verandah with an attendant lady upon either side, preparing a map of the Holy Land, with special reference to the kingdom of the Midianites.' The ear was still very much in Watson's mind at the time when he accompanied Sir Henry Baskerville down to Devonshire in October. Hence the long detailed reports.

The year also produced a good crop of unreported cases. Of these all but one are referred to in *The Hound of the Baskervilles*. The exception is 'Old Abrahams' who was in such mortal terror of his life that Holmes thought it advisable to stay in London and to send Watson to Lausanne. A more interesting event occurred in the month of June when the Pope achieved the distinction of being the only known client to consult Holmes on a second case. Four years earlier it had been in con-nection with the death of Cardinal Tosca[1], this time it was on the subject of the Vatican cameos.

Nor did business show any signs of a recession in the

---

[1] *Black Peter.*

autumn. At the time of *The Hound of the Baskervilles* Holmes was again, ostensibly, detained in London, this time by a case of blackmail which besmirched 'one of the most revered names in England.' This phrase is curiously reminiscent of one which we encountered back in 1886; 'one of the highest, noblest, most exalted names in England.' Was the same person concerned in both cases? If so, one might hazard a guess that the threat of blackmail related to the pawning of 'one of the most precious public possessions of the Empire,' and that the blackmailer was Sir George Burnwell.[1]

Then in November came two more unreported cases. There was first the famous card scandal of the Nonpareil Club in which Holmes exposed the atrocious conduct of Colonel Upwood, thus adding yet another colonel to our already lengthy list, and secondly the defence of the unfortunate Mme Montpensier, accused of murdering her step-daughter, Mlle Carère, who however turned up six months later, alive and married in New York.

And so to 1900 where once again we meet a case which has been dealt with in a previous chapter. This is *The Valley of Fear* which took place in January of that year.[2]

Next on the list comes another 'undated' case, *The Six Napoleons*, on which Mr. Bell has carried out some useful research. He reminds us that the unattractive Italian Beppo went to prison in the year prior to the case, and that the last date on which his wages were paid was May 20th. Our object therefore is to find a year between 1881, when Holmes first came to Baker Street, and 1903, the year

[1] *The Beryl Coronet.*   [2] See pages 111–113.

of his final departure in which May 20th is on a Saturday.

This is reasonable in principle, but at this stage Mr. Bell goes astray, for he omits 1893 which is one of these years and includes 1895 in which May 20th fell on a Monday. In actual fact, the only three years to survive the test are 1882, 1893 and 1899.

Of these, 1893 can be struck out. This is of course one of the Moriarty years, when Holmes was not in Baker Street, so the Prince of Colonna would not have been able to consult him when the black pearl of the Borgias was first stolen. Yet he tells us: 'I was myself consulted upon this case, but I was unable to throw any light upon it.'

Our choice is therefore restricted to 1882 or 1899 as the year of Beppo's arrest, and 1883 or 1900 as the year of *The Six Napoleons*.

The first passage which weights the scales in favour of the later dates is that which contains Lestrade's enthusiastic tribute to Holmes:

'I've seen you handle a good many cases, Mr. Holmes, but I don't know that I ever knew a more workmanlike one than that. We're not jealous of you at Scotland Yard. No, sir, we are very proud of you, and if you come down to-morrow there's not a man, from the oldest inspector to the youngest constable, who wouldn't be glad to shake you by the hand.'

This eulogy does not sound like 1883. It took Holmes a long time to wear down the natural jealousy of the professional for the brilliant amateur. This hostility was for instance still very much in evidence at the time of *The Norwood Builder* in 1894. It seems far more natural to read this tribute as one paid to him at a late stage in his career after his numerous triumphs had compelled Scotland Yard to acknowledge his genius.

Then there is Holmes's remark to Watson: 'If ever I permit you to chronicle any more of my little problems.'

The word 'permit' at once suggests the period after Holmes's return in 1894, for the cases which occurred soon after his return were not published until 1903 or 1904, and it has already been submitted that this was the result of a deliberate veto imposed by Holmes for reasons connected with Colonel Moriarty.[1] There is no evidence of any similar prohibition during the period prior to 1891–1894.

Moreover, if the word 'chronicle' means 'publish,' it would be impossible for Watson to 'chronicle' any more of the cases in 1883, for no case was published earlier than *A Study in Scarlet* in 1887. But it is of course possible that the word refers to the writing of the case as distinct from its actual publication.

Finally the fact that *The Six Napoleons* did not appear in print until 1904 creates fresh difficulties for the 1882–1883 period. Suppose that Holmes had forbidden Watson to 'chronicle' any more cases in 1883. This prohibition must have been withdrawn by 1887 when *A Study in Scarlet* appeared, whilst in the next six years twenty-four other cases were published. Why therefore should *The Six Napoleons* be held over until 1904? It was an exceedingly interesting adventure which ought to have been narrated at the first possible opportunity. The only reason to delay publication of any particular case was that the client might object.[2] But in *The Six Napoleons* there was no client, nor indeed anyone who

[1] See page 122.
[2] As, for example, in the case of *The Speckled Band*.

could possibly object, for this was a case in which Holmes was called in by the police.

To conclude, it appears that the evidence is overwhelmingly against 1882 as the year of Beppo's arrest, and that this event must have actually happened in the last week of May 1899. 'He got off with a year,' and therefore may have come out early in June 1900. He apparently set to work at once to track down the Napoleon statues, and it seems that little time was lost here, for he was helped by a cousin who worked in the firm which made them. We are told that the original trouble culminating in his arrest was 'more than a year ago now' so we do not think we shall be far out if we say that *The Six Napoleons* took place in the late summer of 1900.

At the time of *The Six Napoleons* Holmes was also investigating a forgery case with the somewhat unmelodious name of Conk-Singleton.

In *Thor Bridge* we have once again the familiar situation of a known month in an unknown year. It was on October 3rd that J. Neil Gibson, the Gold King, wrote to Holmes imploring him to take up the case.

Our starting point this time is Billy the page, who, we are told, opened the door and announced Mr. Marlow Bates. Any case which mentions this youngster must be a late one. In point of fact, apart from *Thor Bridge*, he appears only twice, in *The Valley of Fear* (January 1900) and in *The Mazarin Stone* (Summer 1903). In the last mentioned case he is described as 'the young but very wise and tactful page.'

If he was only a young page in the summer of 1903 he can hardly have been a page at all nearly five years earlier, in October 1898. At the other extreme

October 1902 is too late, for by September 3rd of that year Watson had left Baker Street for the last time.[1] This leaves only the Octobers of 1899, 1900 and 1901.

If it be 1899 it falls in the same month as *The Hound of the Baskervilles*. So we must first consider what days in October are required by each case. *Thor Bridge* is straightforward. Holmes and Watson must be in London on the 4th and in Hampshire, either in Winchester or at Thor Bridge on the 5th and 6th. The Baskerville situation is more complicated. Watson's first report from Baskerville Hall near Dartmoor is dated the 13th, but he had been there for some time and had sent Holmes earlier letters and telegrams. He left London by the 10.30 train on a Saturday morning which in 1899 would have to be either September 30th or October 7th. We prefer the earlier date, but either alternative is fatal to the case for 1899 on the grounds that Watson could not be in two places at the same time.

If it be September 30th, he is fairly caught on October 4th with one foot in London and one in Devonshire, whilst on the next two days he is spread-eagled between Hampshire and Devonshire.

Nor is October 7th any better, for they both spent the night of the 6th at the village inn at Thor Bridge which was a short train journey from Winchester, and however early they rose in the morning they would hardly be at Paddington in time to catch the 10.30 train.[2] This appears to dispose of the year 1899.

[1] *The Illustrious Client.*

[2] For those who wish to pursue the matter further, we would point out that there are *at least* three other objections to a combined Thor Bridge-Baskerville week.

1901 can be deleted on account of Holmes's grandiloquent remark to Neil Gibson. 'My professional charges are upon a fixed scale. I do not vary them save when I remit them altogether.' In the case of *The Priory School* which, as we shall see, occurred in May 1901, Holmes received for his services the sum of £6,000, which was paid to him by the Duke of Holdernesse, an austere character who was 'completely immersed in large public questions, and . . . rather inaccessible to all ordinary emotions.' It is true that the initiative came from the Duke, but even so, he would hardly be justified in making the above remark in the month of October after pocketing the Duke's cheque in the month of May.

Accordingly we are left with October 1900 as the only possible date for *Thor Bridge*. The statement was true at the time when Holmes made it, but two factors caused him to change his policy in the following year. The first was the conduct of the Duke, who certainly deserved to pay £6,000. The second was the ruinous extravagance of the Government, which in 1901 raised the rate of income tax from one shilling to one and twopence in the pound. When we recall that *The Priory School* being in the month of May, would come just after the Budget, we realize the significance of Holmes's comment, 'I am a poor man.'

This brings us to the case of *The Priory School* itself. Once again we have no date, but this time there is no real difficulty and all who have previously considered the question have come to the same conclusion. It must be after 1900, for the Duke appeared in Holmes's 'encyclopaedia of reference' as 'Lord-Lieutenant of Hallamshire since 1900.' It also must be in a year in which May 13th falls on a Monday, for Lord Saltire 'was last seen on the night of May 13—that is the night of last Monday.' The only year prior to 1904, when Holmes retired, that meets these requirements is 1901.

To investigate *The Priory School* Holmes had temporarily to suspend his activities on two other important cases, the Ferrers Documents and the Abergavenny Murder, but no further details of these are available. In the following year he refused a knighthood for services which have not yet been disclosed.

After a series of undated cases it is a welcome change to be informed that *The Three Garridebs* occurred in 'the latter end of June 1902.' Lestrade made his final appearance in this case, and it is also the last case reported by Watson before his final departure from Baker Street.

Yet it is not these somewhat melancholy reminders of the march of time that hold our attention in *The Three Garridebs*. There is something very curious about this affair. The crime is a work of art, but the criminal seems to fall below the level of the crime. Could Killer Evans, who appears to be rather a humdrum personality, have invented this very ingenious scheme? It certainly looks as if it were a one-man job, but it may be that the Killer sought out one of his associates, explained his difficulties and asked for advice. The advice was given, the adviser taking care to keep well in the background, so that when the Killer was arrested he escaped. There exists a theory that most criminals repeat certain details every time they commit a crime, so that they may be said to write their signatures across it. If this be so then the signature on *The Three Garridebs* can easily be read. It is one that we have met before, back in the year 1890, in the matter of

The Red-Headed League. It is the signature of the most interesting of all Holmes's opponents, our old acquaintance, John Clay, once of Eton and Oxford, the grandson of a Royal Duke.

Soon after this case Watson left Baker Street and though he paid a few visits to Holmes, he did not reside there again.

Before we leave this period, however, mention should be made of two or three cases referred to incidentally by Watson to which no date can be assigned.

The Veiled Lodger mentions a curious affair which involved a politician, a lighthouse and a trained cormorant. Apparently an attempt had been made to destroy Holmes's papers relating to this matter, but whether the aggressor was the politician, the lighthouse keeper or the trained cormorant is not known.

Then there was that dreadful business of the Abernethy family referred to in *The Six Napoleons*, in which the vital clue was the depth that the parsley had sunk into the butter on a hot day.

Finally we have the list of cases in *Thor Bridge*, comprising the unfortunate Mr. James Phillimore who, stepping back into his house to get his umbrella, was never seen again, the equally unfortunate ship, *Alicia*, which sailed into a patch of mist from which she never emerged, and the case of the well-known journalist and duellist, Isadora Persano, who was found stark staring mad with a match box in front of him containing a remarkable worm, said to be unknown to science.

We confess that we should like to know more about this remarkable worm. One could almost stock a menagerie with the strange creatures encountered by Holmes from time to time about which we know all too little. In addition to the worm it would include the repulsive red leech which was presumably responsible for the death of Crosby the banker,[1] the giant rat of Sumatra which haunted the good ship *Matilda Briggs*[2] and of course the trained cormorant.

[1] *The Golden Pince-Nez.*
[2] *The Sussex Vampire.*

CHAPTER FIFTEEN

My Dear Mrs. Watson the Second

WATSON was still at Baker Street in June 1902 at the time of *The Three Garridebs*, but he had left before the 3rd September of that year, which is the opening date of the case of *The Illustrious Client*. There is no mystery this time as to why he left. It was for the purpose of getting married again. It would seem, however, that the marriage had not taken place by September, for he tells us that 'I was living in my own rooms in Queen Anne Street at the time.'

The evidence for this further matrimonial adventure is contained in *The Blanched Soldier*, a case which occurred 'in January, 1903, just after the conclusion of the Boer War,' so the marriage would probably be some time in the last quarter of 1902.

Watson having departed, *The Blanched Soldier* purports to be written by Holmes himself. Whether or not this conclusion can be accepted is a matter for further consideration, but in any event there is no reason to doubt that it gives an authentic account of his views on the second Mrs. Watson.

They were not exactly flattering. According to him, 'the good Watson had at that time deserted me for a wife, the only selfish action which I can recall in our association.'

Somehow or other this does not seem to be an entirely logical or consistent remark to make on a second marriage as distinct from a first. Some explanation appears to be required, but this can be deferred until we have dealt with the rest of the events of the year 1903.

Holmes tells us that at the time of *The Blanched Soldier* he had a commission from the Sultan of Turkey, involving political consequences of the gravest kind, and also that he was still clearing up 'the case which my friend Watson has described as that of the Abbey School in which the Duke of Greyminster was so deeply involved.' But in point of fact his friend Watson had described the case of the Priory School in which the Duke of Holdernesse was so deeply involved. Are we then to budget for two schools and two Dukes, or merely one of each? This, too, is a problem to be considered at a later stage.

The next two cases, *The Mazarin Stone* and *The Three Gables* have some features in common. Watson is paying a visit to his old home on each occasion. *The Mazarin Stone* is on 'the evening of a lovely summer's day,' whilst *The Three Gables* would also appear to be in the summer since there is reference to geranium beds.

In each case the possible periods for such a visit are 1888–90, 1896, and 1902–03. Of these 1896 can be excluded for both cases, if the theory of a quarrel between Holmes and Watson in that year is accepted.[1]

So far as *The Mazarin Stone* is concerned 1888–90 can be excluded, since Watson tells Billy the page about the booby trap which was set for Colonel Sebastian Moran in 1894.

Nor can it be 1902, for he was still actually living in Baker Street as late as the end of June in that year at

[1] See Chapter XIII.

the time of *The Three Garridebs*, but the visit in *The Mazarin Stone* is clearly made after a fairly long absence. This is evident both from his conversation with Billy, and from Holmes's remark, 'you bear every sign of the busy medical man, with calls on him every hour.' He has had time to build up a practice. It follows, therefore, that the lovely summer evening must have been in the year 1903.

The same procedure can now be applied to *The Three Gables*. There are two reasons for preferring the 1902–03 period to 1888–90.

First there is the reference to the journalist with the rugged name of Langdale Pike (an appropriate name, incidentally, to find in a case referred to as The Three Gables) who made a 'Four-figure income by the paragraphs which he contributed every week to the garbage papers which cater for an inquisitive public.' This certainly sounds more like the later period. By 1890 the popular press was still in its infancy. It is highly unlikely that in those days a journalist would be able to earn a four-figure income by contributing society paragraphs.

Secondly, *The Three Gables* is one of the dozen cases which appear in *The Case Book of Sherlock Holmes*. All the other cases in *The Case Book* occur after Holmes's return. In some there may be doubt as to the exact year, but so far it has never been suggested by anyone that any of them are earlier than 1894, and there is no reason at all why *The Three Gables* should be the one exception to this rule.

Having excluded 1888–90, there only remains the choice between 1902 and 1903. The summer of 1902 is a possibility, but the time is somewhat limited, for as we have already observed, Watson was still living in Baker Street at the end of June, i.e. at the time of *The Three Garridebs*. If *The Three Gables* occurred at the end of that summer one might reasonably expect him to state that he had recently changed his abode. In fact, he makes no reference to this. All that he says is: 'I had not seen Holmes for some days.'

It would appear therefore that *The Three Gables* can be assigned to the summer of 1903, and that it must be *after* and not *before* *The Mazarin Stone*, so as to fit in with the long absence which preceded that case.

The only remaining case for the year 1903 is *The Creeping Man* which took place early in September, and as this was 'one of the very last cases handled by Holmes before his retirement from practice,' it is probable that his final exit from Baker Street occurred at the end of 1903.

The departure of Watson may well have been the reason which caused Holmes to retire. Once again it was a case of: 'I am lost without my Boswell.'[1] Only this time there was a different 'Mrs. Boswell' in the picture.

Practically no information is available as to the identity of the second Mrs. Watson. Mr. S. C. Roberts has suggested that she was the former Violet de Merville, the heroine of *The Illustrious Client*, but Mr. Blakeney has produced eight arguments against this theory, of which the most conclusive is that Watson does not know who enlightened her as to the true character of Baron Gruner, a fact of which he could hardly be in ignorance if he had married her. It is equally unlikely that he married any of the other unattached ladies referred to in his narratives. A strong case can be made against any one of them.

[1] *A Scandal in Bohemia.*

All that we can deduce about the lady is that she did not inspire any enthusiasm in Holmes. This is apparent from his statement in *The Blanched Soldier* previously quoted, that 'the good Watson had at that time deserted me for a wife, the only selfish action which I can recall in our association.' Evidently Holmes did not like her.

In these circumstances one might have expected a similar outburst from him at the time of the first marriage. But apparently his relations with the first Mrs. Watson were amicable, for on his reunion with Watson on the occasion of *The Stockbroker's Clerk*, he asked after her, and expressed the hope that she had quite recovered from her experiences in *The Sign of Four*. It seems, therefore, that he did not object to all Mrs. Watsons on principle, but merely to this particular Mrs. Watson.

There can be little doubt as to the cause of the trouble. Watson, after both his marriages, tried to ride two horses at the same time. One horse was his medical practice, the other, the job of acting as recorder of Sherlock Holmes. With feminine realism both Mrs. Watsons saw the danger of this circus act. Each was in favour of a single horse, but they differed in their choice.

The first wife thought that her husband's true vocation was to act as Holmes's historian. Never mind his practice. Anstruther or Jackson or anyone else suitable could look after that. The result was that the practice languished,[1] but Watson was given every possible encouragement by his wife to visit Holmes. He looked pale and needed a change.[2] She was visiting her aunt.[3]

---

[1] 'I have nothing to do to-day. My practice is never very absorbing.' *The Red-Headed League.*

[2] *The Boscombe Valley Mystery.*   [3] *The Five Orange Pips.*

The client was an old schoolfellow, so Watson must accompany him.[1] At any time of the day[2] or night[3] he would forsake everything, and with a hurried message to his wife would dash off to join Holmes. His wife never complained. Obviously this was just the sort of Mrs. Watson to suit Sherlock Holmes.

The second Mrs. Watson, on the other hand, took the reverse view. A substantial practice was built up within a year,[4] but the visits to Holmes were very few. She did not demand a complete break with Holmes. To suggest that would be an exaggeration. But in her view such visits should be for social purposes only. Watson would be wasting his time if he accompanied Holmes on his adventures or wrote up his cases. Naturally this was just the sort of Mrs. Watson *not* to suit Sherlock Holmes. Hence his acid remark on Watson's selfishness in marrying her.

As we have already seen, four cases are recorded in 1903, the year that followed the marriage, *The Blanched Soldier*, *The Mazarin Stone*, *The Three Gables*, and *The Creeping Man*. Of these only the last two are ostensibly written by Watson. He takes part in *The Mazarin Stone*, but the narrative is written in the third person, whilst *The Blanched Soldier* apparently occurred in his absence, Holmes purporting to be the writer on this occasion.

The authorship of these two cases appears to require investigation. Were they, in fact, written by Holmes? Or by Watson? Or by some third party?

It seems clear that our starting point must be Mrs.

---

[1] *The Naval Treaty.*   [2] *The Stockbroker's Clerk.*
[3] *The Man with the Twisted Lip.*
[4] 'You bear every sign of the busy medical man, with calls on him every hour.'   *The Mazarin Stone.*

Watson's attitude towards her husband's co-operation with Holmes. As soon as she discovered that Watson had written *The Three Gables* and *The Creeping Man* she put a stop to any further writing, and Watson either obeyed her or deceived her. The second alternative seems the more probable.

That Holmes was the author on either occasion seems highly improbable. Even if he knew that Watson's services were no longer available, it seems very unlikely that he would start to record his cases at this stage in his career. We know that many interesting cases had come his way in the three years prior to his meeting with Watson,[1] and there must have been others when Watson was away in 1896. But he never seems to have thought it worth while to write an account of any of these. For that matter there were many more cases not dealt with by Watson during the years when Watson was living with him, which Holmes might have recorded if he had felt disposed to do so. Why, then, at this late stage in his career should he take it into his head to narrate two not particularly interesting cases?

Moreover, if he were the author the style would surely be quite different. Holmes thought that Watson pandered too much to popular taste, instead of confining himself strictly to the bare facts. It is true, of course, that the author of *The Blanched Soldier* had realized this, and there is an admission by Holmes that, after all, Watson was right and that he had at last realized that a more popular approach was necessary. But this is not very convincing. It does not sound like Holmes. It sounds far more like Watson trying to think of an excuse for writing in his usual style.

[1] *The Musgrave Ritual.*

There remains the possibility that they were written by a third party. He would have to be someone to whom Holmes had related the two episodes, as he was apparently not present on either occasion. There appears to be no very obvious candidate for this post. Nor is there any apparent reason why any third party should pretend to be Holmes in *The Blanched Soldier*, though there was a perfectly good reason for Watson to do so. Nor, again, is there any reason why he should write in a style which bears such a close resemblance to Watson's.

The probability is therefore that Watson was the author of both narratives. After Mrs. Watson had expressed her displeasure that he was still acting as Holmes's recorder, he came to the conclusion that disguise was essential. His first experiment was to write *The Mazarin Stone* in the third person. But this did not satisfy him, or her. It was too negative, and even if he were acquitted of the charge of authorship, he was still open to the accusation that he had wasted his time by accompanying Holmes on the case.

So the deception was carried a further stage in *The Blanched Soldier*, which purports to be written by Holmes in Watson's absence. He found it difficult, however, to abandon his usual method of presenting a case, and so 'Holmes' had to pretend that he had modified his views on this. As an additional smoke screen 'Holmes' could refer to one of the cases previously recorded by Watson, and in doing so he could go astray in the names, thus supplying further evidence that Watson was not the author. Hence we get 'The Abbey School' instead of 'The Priory School' and 'the Duke of Greyminster' instead of 'the Duke of Holdernesse.'

Before making our final departure from Baker Street a word may perhaps be said on Watson's statement in *The Veiled Lodger* that 'Mr. Sherlock Holmes was in active practice for twenty-three years . . . and during seventeen of these I was allowed to co-operate with him and to keep notes of his doings.'

So far as Holmes's twenty-three years are concerned the situation is straightforward. Thirteen of them were from 1878 to 1890 inclusive and the remaining ten were from 1894 to 1903 inclusive.

Six of these twenty-three years must be deducted in order to arrive at Watson's seventeen. Three of the six are clearly 1878 to 1880, the period prior to their first meeting. The remaining three, it is suggested, are 1881, 1896, and 1903. A word of explanation may be necessary in each case.

1881. In *The Five Orange Pips* Watson refers to 'my notes and records of the Sherlock Holmes' cases between the years '82 and '90.' He excludes '81, the first year in Baker Street, and this should cause no surprise for he had not joined forces with Holmes for the purpose of acting as Holmes's recorder. Indeed, when they first met he was ignorant of Holmes's occupation. The idea of a general record of the cases would naturally occur to him only gradually. Probably he spent most of 1881 in slowly writing up *A Study in Scarlet*, without informing Holmes or obtaining his permission. It is unlikely that he took notes of any other case during that year. At the end of the year he approached Holmes with his idea. Holmes agreed, and a definite arrangement was made whereby Watson was to narrate the more interesting cases. On this basis 1881 would rightly be excluded.

1896. This, it will be recalled, was the occasion when

Watson was away from Baker Street for the greater part of the year. He was still there at its commencement and he returned in November so, strictly speaking, the entire year ought not to be excluded. But one need not look for too minute a degree of accuracy in a statement of this nature.

1903. In fact he was still co-operating with Holmes in 1903, but officially this had to be concealed to avoid incurring the displeasure of Mrs. Watson.

The twenty-three years had run their course and Baker Street was now a thing of the past. But it was not the end. Adventure had not yet deserted Sherlock Holmes.

CHAPTER SIXTEEN

His Last Bow

HOLMES is next encountered in his villa 'situated on the southern slope of the Downs, commanding a great view of the Channel.' The exact location of the villa is not known, but from the above description it must be somewhere in that part of the Downs which stretches from Brighton to Eastbourne.

He had retired there to take up bee-farming with the result that some years later the world was enriched by the publication of a *Practical Handbook of Bee Culture, with some Observations upon the Segregation of the Queen.*

His sole companion was 'my old housekeeper.' The word 'old' is ambiguous, but it may mean that the lady referred to is his erstwhile landlady, Mrs. Hudson, a faithful retainer, who adorned 221B Baker Street as early as 1883[1] and as late as 1903.[2]

In July 1907 there occurred the episode of *The Lion's Mane.* This, like *The Blanched Soldier,* purports to be written by Holmes in Watson's absence, but once again the style is unmistakably Watsonian, and there can be no doubt as to the authorship. Watson at this time used to pay 'an occasional week-end visit' to Holmes, and it would be on one of these occasions that Holmes supplied him with the material to write his account of the case.

The next five years were uneventful and Holmes

[1] *The Speckled Band.*   [2] *The Mazarin Stone.*

was quite content to spend his time studying his bees, 'watching the little working gangs as once I watched the criminal world of London.' But the first shadows of war were already on the horizon. In 1912 Sir Edward Grey came down to Sussex. His eloquence was insufficient and reinforcement by Mr. Asquith was necessary before Holmes could be uprooted. A master spy was at work, who time and again had proved to be a jump ahead of our own Secret Service.

It took Holmes two years to overthrow this Moriarty of espionage. In the interval he had to travel far: to Chicago, to Buffalo, to Skibbareen. The climax came on August 2, 1914, as narrated in *His Last Bow*. The ever faithful Watson was in at the kill. His wife could not object on this occasion for he was combating the enemies of his country.

We come to our last glimpse of the two friends. They are looking out on the moonlit sea at Harwich. Their task has been successfully accomplished. The master spy has been arrested. But war within the next few hours is inevitable. Holmes gazes thoughtfully out to sea.

'There's an east wind coming, Watson.'

'I think not, Holmes. It is very warm.'

'Good old Watson! You are the one fixed point in a changing age.'

There, alas we must leave them. One would like to have known what happened afterwards. Holmes probably spent the next four years in unmasking German spies, a task for which he was obviously well-equipped. Thereafter we imagine that he returned once more to his bees on the Sussex Downs and that he is still there to-day. For he bears a charmed life. If ever a man was immortal, that man was Sherlock Holmes.

APPENDIX I

Chronological Table

FOR quick reference the dates of the sixty cases reported at length, and certain other dates, are here recorded.

	1846	Mycroft Holmes born.
	1853	Sherlock Holmes born.
	1871	Holmes goes up to Oxford.
August–September	1873	*The 'Gloria Scott.'*
	1876	Holmes comes down from Oxford and takes rooms in Montague Street.
	1878	*The Musgrave Ritual.*
January	1881	Holmes and Watson meet.
March	1881	*A Study in Scarlet.*
March	1882	*The Yellow Face.*
Summer	1882	*The Greek Interpreter.*
December	1882	*Charles Augustus Milverton.*
April	1883	*The Speckled Band.*
March	1886	*The Beryl Coronet.*
Autumn	1886	*The Second Stain.*
April	1887	*The Reigate Squires.*
July	1887	*The Sign of Four.*
August	1887	*The Cardboard Box.*
September–October	1887	*Silver Blaze.*
October (early)	1887	*The Noble Bachelor.*
October (late)	1887	*The Resident Patient.*
November	1887	Watson marries Miss Morstan.
June	1888	*The Stockbroker's Clerk.*
July	1888	*The Naval Treaty.*
August	1888	*The Crooked Man.*
September	1888	*The Five Orange Pips.*
March	1889	*A Scandal in Bohemia.*
April	1889	*A Case of Identity.*
June (early)	1889	*The Boscombe Valley Mystery.*
June (late)	1889	*The Man with the Twisted Lip.*
July or August	1889	*The Engineer's Thumb.*

November	1889	*The Dying Detective.*
December	1889	*The Blue Carbuncle.*
March	1890	*The Copper Beeches.*
October	1890	*The Red-Headed League.*
April	1891	*The Final Problem.*
April–February	1891 1894	The Moriarty interval.
February	1894	*The Empty House.*
March	1894	*Wisteria Lodge.*
May	1894	*Shoscombe Old Place.*
August	1894	*The Norwood Builder.*
November	1894	*The Gold Pince-Nez.*
April	1895	*The Solitary Cyclist.*
May	1895	*The Three Students.*
July	1895	*Black Peter.*
November	1895	*The Bruce-Partington Plans.*
January	1896	*The Red Circle.*
	1896	In Watson's absence Holmes starts the Sherlock Holmes Agency.
November	1896	Watson returns.
November (early)	1896	*The Veiled Lodger.*
November (late)	1896	*The Sussex Vampire.*
January	1897	*The Abbey Grange.*
March	1897	*The Devil's Foot.*
December	1897	*The Missing Three-Quarter.*
Summer	1898	*The Retired Colourman.*
July–August	1898	*The Dancing Men.*
Summer	1899	*Lady Frances Carfax.*
October	1899	*The Hound of the Baskervilles.*
January	1900	*The Valley of Fear.*
Summer (late)	1900	*The Six Napoleons.*
October	1900	*Thor Bridge.*
May	1901	*The Priory School.*
June	1902	*The Three Garridebs.*
Summer (late)	1902	Watson leaves Baker Street.
September	1902	*The Illustrious Client.*
Autumn	1902	Watson's second marriage.
January	1903	*The Blanched Soldier.*
Summer	1903	*The Mazarin Stone.*
Summer	1903	*The Three Gables.*
September	1903	*The Creeping Man.*

Autumn	1903	Holmes retires from Baker Street to Sussex.
July	1907	*The Lion's Mane*.
	1912	At the urgent request of the Prime Minister, Holmes commences his two years' campaign against Von Bork.
August	1914	*His Last Bow*.

APPENDIX II

The Bibliography of Sherlock Holmes

Before March 1881   *On the Distinction between the Ashes of the Various Tobaccos.*

A monograph enumerating 140 varieties of cigar, cigarette, and pipe tobacco, with coloured plates illustrating the difference in the ash. This was probably Holmes's first and favourite child. He continually refers to it. (*A Study in Scarlet, The Sign of Four, The Boscombe Valley Mystery.*)

March 1881   *The Book of Life.*

An article in a magazine on the science of observation and deduction. (*A Study in Scarlet.*)

March 1886   *On Variations in the Human Ear.*

Two short monographs in the *Anthropological Journal.* (*The Cardboard Box.*)

Before July 1887   *On the Tracing of Footsteps.*

A monograph containing, *inter alia,* some remarks on the use of plaster of Paris as a preserver of impresses. (*The Sign of Four.*)

Before July 1887   *The influence of a Trade upon the Form of the Hand.*

Containing lithotypes of hands of slaters, sailors, cork-cutters, compositors, weavers, and diamond polishers. (*The Sign of Four.*)

Before October 1890   *On Tattoo Marks.*

It is probable that this is one of Holmes's earliest works and that his interest in this subject dates back to his undergraduate days when he made his first successful deduction from the tattoo marks on the elder Trevor's arm. (*The Red-Headed League.*)

Probably 1896	*The Polyphonic Motets of Lassus.*
	A monograph printed for private circulation and said by the experts to be the last word on the subject. (*The Bruce-Partington Plans.*)
Before July 1897	*On Secret Writings.*
	A monograph which analyses one hundred and sixty separate ciphers. (*The Dancing Men.*)
Before October 1899	*On the Dating of Documents.*
	A brief monograph. (*The Hound of the Baskervilles.*)
Between 1904 and 1912	*The Practical Handbook of Bee Culture with some Observations upon the Segregation of the Queen.*
	The *magnum opus* of Holmes's later years. "The fruit of pensive nights and laborious days." (*His Last Bow.*)

THE END